FROM COAL MINE UPWARDS

Jas. Dunn

FROM COAL MINE UPWARDS

OR,

Seventy Years of an Eventful Life

BY

JAMES DUNN,

Author of "Modern London," &c., &c.

WITH NUMEROUS ILLUSTRATIONS.

W. GREEN,

3, BRIDEWELL PLACE, LONDON, E.C.

To

The ever blessed memory

of

My dear departed Wife,

who,

for nearly thirty years,

shared my joys and sorrows

and

who was a true helpmeet

in the

toils and triumphs of the Gospel,

I dedicate this book.

PREFACE.

THE life of a "self-made" man must always be interesting. No man can raise himself in the social scale, especially if his early life be passed under great disadvantages, unless he has marked qualities, such as determination, pluck, patience, and principle.

The autobiography of Mr. Dunn not only demonstrates the truth of this statement, but has this additional interest, that it shows how a poor working lad may, through the Grace of God being brought to bear on a strong character, become an earnest and successful worker for the good of his fellowman, and for the glory of his Lord and Saviour. I heartily commend the book to all who are interested in the advance of the Kingdom of God upon earth.

F. A. BEVAN.

January, 1910.

AUTHOR'S FOREWORD.

FOR a number of years past I have been urged by different friends to write an account of my life, but I did not think that it was worth while troubling the public with the story of my poor chequered career.

As time went on these requests were repeatedly made, and I began to wonder whether I ought not to accede to them, but it was not until my late good friend, the Rev. Robert Dawson, B.A., Secretary of the London City Mission, seriously wished me to commence the task without delay, lest I should be called Home before it was accomplished, that I thought of penning the following lines.

In recalling memories of the past seventy years, from the coal mine until now, I have had mingled feelings of pleasure and pain, of joy and sorrow, of thankfulness and regret.

I have sought in the following pages to depict both the light and shade of my life, and while in my younger days, and also in later years, I had to endure privations and pass through seasons of stress and storm, still the brightness and joy of my life far outweigh the sorrow and pain, and I can say with the Psalmist, "goodness and mercy" have followed me all my days.

It was necessary in compressing a career of seventy years into this volume, to omit some things that might have been written, and so I have sought chiefly to describe those periods of my life, and the scenes that I passed through, which I thought might be interesting and helpful to the reader. For myself the review of seven decades has confirmed my faith in God, not only as a Being of boundless grace to the most unworthy and abandoned, as the narrative shows, but also as a God of Providence, over-ruling the events of a life and making the most trivial thing to accomplish some important end. Some of the most serious things that happened to me in the far past, and which at the time seemed overwhelmingly disastrous, and from which I could see no possible way of escape, have been so over-ruled for my good, that but for those very calamities I cannot see how I could have been brought to my present position.

If these experiences, as recorded in the following pages, should lead my young readers to trust in God in the darkest hours of their early manhood, and wait patiently and trustfully, while watching for the guiding of His providence; if they should help the middle aged to manfully perform the duties of life, however severe the strain or long the duration; to lead them to cast their burden on the Lord and wait for His deliverance, which is sure to come and which never comes too late; if they should comfort the aged in the evening of life, and brighten their hopes of the Home of happy reunions in the land beyond, then the end will be answered which led me to write this book in addition to my ordinary duties, and which, although so imperfectly put together, may, I trust, be used of God for the extension of His Kingdom.

May I ask the sympathy and forbearance of the kind reader for any mistakes or discrepancies that may be found in the book?

And now asking the forgiveness of God for anything which has been written not in accordance with His Holy Will, to Him, Father, Son, and Holy Ghost, be ascribed all glory now and for ever.—*Amen.*

J.D.

PROLOGUE.

OVER sixty years ago in a small village south of Charley Forest, on the border of the Leicestershire coalfields, a company of men (consisting of the vicar and several of the principal farmers and leading tradesmen of the place) met in the old vicarage to discuss a question—to some perhaps of little consequence, to others (among them the vicar) a question of some importance, but to the one most concerned (who knew nothing of the proceedings till years afterwards) it had momentous issues.

The question was, what was to be done with a poor lad eight years old, who had received all the education then possible from the two school teachers of the village, the "old dame," and the "shoe-maker." The vicar, who presided, and several others were desirous that the lad should be sent to a school in the county town to be further educated, with a view to fitting him for some useful position in life, possibly that of village schoolmaster.

The arguments used were many and varied, the principal one being that the lad had shown signs of diligence, having carried away many of the little prizes both in the day and Sunday School, and manifested a desire for knowledge. Everything up to this point appeared to be in the lad's favour.

There was one person, however, who had not expressed his views, and as he was the most important person there his opinion would have the greatest weight. Although very illiterate—not being able to read or write—he was the richest farmer in the neighbourhood, having by his success in farming, and cattle-breeding, acquired considerable wealth and influence. He said,

"I should like to ask two questions before you decide, the first is, how much learning does it want to drive the plough?" Of course, the chairman had to admit that it required very little, if any.

The other question was,

"How much learning does it need for a lad to work in the coal-pit?" That question was answered in the same way as the first one.

"Then," he said, emphatically, "my decision is that he at once goes to work at one or the other."

"That," as a man told me some years after—for I was the lad—"settled the matter," and to the coal-pit at eight years of age I was sent to work. It was in those dismal mines, four hundred yards deep and about one mile under ground from the bottom of the shaft, that I commenced to earn my daily bread. But the eye of God was over me, and in due time He delivered me from the pit, as will be seen hereafter.

CONTENTS.

LIST OF ILLUSTRATIONS.

FROM COAL MINE UPWARDS.

FIRST DECADE.

THE history of the first ten years of my life was a varied one, and during the latter part of the period I passed through great hardships. I was born in a village south of Charley Forest, on the border of the Leicestershire coalfields. The year of my birth, 1835, was the year in which the London City Mission was founded, and in the service of that Society I have spent the greater portion of my life.

At the time of my birth my parents were in very comfortable circumstances, my father being a civil engineer and contractor. He had carried out some important works under "Brunel," the great French engineer, and completed the first Thames tunnel, after it had been flooded by the water breaking through, and left for a long time in that state.

In course of time my father took a contract on the railway which was to be constructed from Leicester to Whitwick coalfields, as an outlet for the vast resources of coal found in the north-west part of the county. About ten miles from the town where it started, and in the parish where I first saw the light, there was what appeared to be an insuperable difficulty in the matter of a very steep gradient of about one and a quarter miles long. In those days they had not the high pressure engines which we have now, to climb the incline from the low level to the higher one of the coalfield district. In order to meet this difficulty, my father constructed a very strong revolving drum—or cylinder, fixed at the top of the slope with a stout rope, the length of the incline, passing round it, the upper end being fastened to a number of full coal waggons, and the lower end being hooked on to some empty waggons. At a given signal the full ones were started over the brow, and began to move downwards, thus pulling the empty ones up. The working of this incline was very dangerous to the brakesmen, and it was no uncommon event for one of them to be maimed—or even killed.

The above system was in operation for some years when it was superseded by a new line from Leicester to Burton-on-Trent.

Many years afterwards I was walking down the old incline—which was then used as a road—when I thought of him who was brought there to carry out the undertaking, and, although it was now discarded, yet I doubted not that it was an important link in the chain by which Divine Providence so ordered events that my parents were married and I was born during its construction.

MY MOTHER.

My mother was a native of the place and came of a sturdy stock, who had lived on the south side of the hills for generations. All her brothers and sisters were tall and strongly built—most of the men being 6 ft. or more in height—and some of them had served their country in the Peninsular wars (one being at Waterloo with Wellington), for they were fine horsemen.

Some time after my birth, the nurse noticed a protuberance on my right side, and it caused no little concern to my parents. I would not refer to it, only that it was afterwards an important factor under God, in shaping my future; and, as I grew, the swelling also became larger.

THE PRIZE-FIGHTING RING.

Before I was three years old my father had become an inveterate drinker, and having a pretty good income he found plenty of companions. He was a great supporter of the '' Prize Fighting Ring,'' which was then at the height of its brutal fame. He attended most of the '' heavy-weight '' matches, and was a great financial supporter of several. I cannot remember him, for he died when I was a very small boy—I believe through the effects of strong drink—leaving my mother a penniless widow, with two little boys to provide for (the youngest being a child in arms).

The village schoolmaster used to tell me of my father's splendid abilities, and of his having been a

Dublin University man, but all this only added to the bitterness of my childhood, during which I have watched my mother work, and weep, while striving to earn a precarious living for her fatherless boys. In after years, I always felt a yearning pity for a boy who had a drunken father, as I had passed through untold sorrow from the same cause.

POVERTY AND AFFLICTION.

As a boy I had to endure a great deal—not only from privation, and want, through being underfed, and scantily clothed—but also from being afflicted with the tumour, which, as I have mentioned, appeared soon after birth. These things excited pity in some hearts, but the opposite feelings in others, for in the early years of my life, my lot was cast—for the greater part—among an ignorant and brutalized people !

LOW WAGES AND DEAR FOOD.

In those days wages were very low, and food very dear, and several wet harvests made the lot of the poor distressing in the extreme. Wheaten bread could not be purchased by the agricultural labourers, whose weekly wages averaged about nine shillings, and out of that they had to feed and clothe a family, and pay rent. Barley bread, with a few potatoes and turnips, formed the staple food of the poor.

Wheat was at famine price, and farmers who were able to hold back their stocks for a year or two, almost made fortunes ! Strange though it may seem, I well remember hearing of certain farmers, who had large farms, some of whose labourers had families in a starving condition, hoarding up the corn in granaries or rick-yards, when the starvation of the poor, their prayers, or even their curses, would not induce them to part with their hoards, as they were certain that the price would still rise, although as I have said, it was at famine height.

THE TRADES OF THE COUNTRY.

The staple trade of the country town was hosiery, mainly manufactured by handlooms, and in many of the villages around. Both men and women—commonly called " stockingers "—had these looms or " stocking frames " in their houses, either owning them, or more generally hiring them from the manufacturer. About this time—(before the corn-laws were repealed)—in addition to the high price of breadstuffs, through wet harvests, and the terrible potato disease, there was a great scarcity of work in the hosiery trade, and thousands of families in consequence were in dire distress. I well remember how companies of poor men, and their wives and children, used to go through the villages singing their poverty wail-songs, the refrain of one (which I cannot forget) being :—

" To hear the children cry for bread,
" What parent can endure? "

The famine-stricken agricultural people would share their scant meal-food, their vegetables and sometimes their pence with these stockingers, while in the colliery villages they would fare better. This terrible state of things drove many a man to acts of desperation; robberies of all kinds were frequent, and many persons got transported for sheep-stealing, etc., while some committed murder when attempting to rob, and were hanged.

SCHOOL DAYS.

My school days—for the greater part, at least—were hard times for me. Most days I felt the pangs of hunger; our usual food consisted of gruel, potatoes and bread with occasionally a little bacon—and but a scant supply of that. This kind of daily living was not very helpful or stimulating to a boy in his endeavour to master his lessons. I persevered however, and was helped by the schoolmaster, the kind clergyman of the village, and the private tutor to his family. My poor mother plied her needle almost night and day—for she was skilful at making certain garments—and I helped as best I could before and after school hours. I well remember how eagerly I would run on an errand, however far it was, to earn a few coppers to help to procure our daily food. Sometimes it was a journey of a few miles, and if it should be to the house of a gentleman or a generous farmer, I would get a good meal, which was eagerly accepted. I also helped, as well as I was able, in the harvest time, and would be up early enough week-day mornings to call men up, in time for them to be at their work by 6 o'clock. I assisted my " shoe-maker " schoolmaster, who was also parish clerk, grave digger, choir master, overseer, and in fact filled almost every post in the village. Thus, in a variety of ways I used often to get food, and sometimes pence to help the home-board. Sometimes on waking I found my mother weeping, when she was still working by the light of a thin candle far into the night. I did not know the cause of her tears, as she gazed into my face, but I learned afterwards for an eminent physician had assured her that my affliction must bring about my death, at the age of 9 or 10 years.

TO THE COAL-PIT.

The crisis was reached, however, as I have described at the beginning of this book, and I shall never forget my mother preparing my little garments for the "mine." A flannel shirt, with wide trousers, a cap, a smock-frock—all made of flannel—while the shoe-maker supplied the usual heavy nailed shoes. The distance from home to the pits was about two miles. I had to have my breakfast of gruel, etc., before five o'clock, so as to be at the pithead by six.

My wages were at the rate of tenpence a day, but as the colliers seldom worked more than half-days, my week's wages rarely came to more than " two shillings and sixpence."

LIFE IN A MINE.

With most lads it was considered a day to be proud of, when they first started to work in a regular way.

I was about the smallest boy who went from our village to the mines, but on the first morning, as I trudged along in my clean flannel suit, with my little bag and bottle round my neck containing the little " pasty " for my day's food, and some weak tea to drink, my feelings were strangely mingled with hope and fear.

After the pit's company had all assembled at the " bank," candles and other equipments having been served out, the descent began. As a rule the boys were sent down first—not in " cages," as is the case in these days, but swinging in chains, a certain number descending at one time. A number of chains were attached to a large ring at the top end, and at the end of a single chain several feet long a double chain forming a loop finishing it. Into one of these loops each person put his legs, and gathering the chain up round his thighs passed it over his left arm, the little company standing in a circle, the left arm with the chain over it in the centre, and the right on the outside free. As the engine lifted them up off the bridge, the chains being of equal lengths, they formed a ring, sitting almost in each other's laps, and the left arm being round the chain on the inside made it very difficult, if not altogether impossible for any one person to fall out.

I can never forget that first morning, as I was shown how to place myself in the chain, and the awful suspense of waiting—only a few seconds—to be drawn up, so that the bridge could be slid from over the shaft, and

A COLLIER LAD.

the descent began. As I went down into the darkness I closed my eyes for very fear, and I think that if ever a lad prayed in earnest, I did so during that, my first descent into the bowels of the earth. I thought of my little home, my poor mother, my Sunday School, wondering if I should be permitted to see them again, and asked God to protect me from accident and death.

IN THE DARKNESS.

We were soon at the bottom, and with candles lighted —for naked lights could be used in these mines—started on our march to the face of the coal-seam where our work lay. I had to divest myself of all clothing except my short flannel trousers, boots and stockings and my flannel skull cap for the air was very warm being so far from the shaft. The man with whom I had to work showed me how to place a leathern belt round my loins, with a light chain attached about a yard long, which was hooked to the front of the small waggon of coals thus pulling in the front while the man pushed behind. In this way I began my first real work, or slavery, for it was nothing less than *child slavery*.

HARDSHIPS.

It was not long before my poor little body was sore with the belt, as also from the stripes laid on the naked back by the hardened cruel miner. I cannot say how many times I cried that first day—aye, and on many days afterwards—but, as is mostly the case, time inures one to almost any kind of hardship.

These mines were owned by a nobleman, who also owned the land and several villages around. The coal was worked out by a few *expert* miners—who were termed " Butties "—at so much a ton, the same being weighed as the waggons were sent off by rail, or by the many kinds of conveyances (by what was termed " land-sale "), from the farmer's large waggons, drawn by three or four horses, down to the poor donkey who carried its load in " paniers," or the man who took away a little in hand-truck or barrow. Then the " Butties " sublet most of the working out of the coal to other miners—such as the " holing," or under-mining of the coal-seam, which was paid for at so much a " stint," this being two yards in length on the coal face, and one yard underneath. They also sublet to the latter the bringing out of the coal from the face of the seam to the pit-bank, at so much per ton, and it was these latter miners who employed the boys, and upon whom they so frequently seemed to delight in displaying their brutal ferocity.

The coal was brought from the face of the seam to the bottom of the shaft in small trucks, and this process was worked in what they called " stages," or lengths, a man having one stage, and then two boys the next, then another miner and then two boys, and this was continued throughout the whole length. Now it will be seen that every pair of boys were running between two men—one at each end of their stage—and the great concern of the boys was to meet the man at either end, so as not to keep them waiting, which was often an impossible task, for if the boys had to wait for the full truck at the one end, the man at the other end would be waiting with his empty truck, and the probability was the boys would be beaten with his strap, and if it was the reverse way then they would meet with the same brutal treatment at the other end. As I have said, collier lads in time became quite inured to this cruel treatment, but to beginners, like myself, it was painful in the extreme. Those who were more hardened would curse and swear, and perhaps wreak their young vengeance on the weaker lads—and such was I, and so was compelled to slave, to suffer and cry the day through.

HALF A DAY'S WORK.

The " turning "—as it was called—that is the bringing up of the coal from the bottom of the shaft to the bank, was done in what the men termed half-days, that is six hours of time. It was seldom they turned a full day of twleve hours, but that did not matter to the men, as they worked " piece-work," but what of the collier lads, what did it mean to them? Well, let me try and explain. As has been seen, the boys were sent down into the mine first, about six o'clock in the morning, and they tramped underground to their respective places of work. As soon as the men were all down, and the "loaders" reached the face, they began to fill the trucks, which were then taken from stage to stage to the bottom of the shaft, and built up on the skep, and when that skep reached the bank, the time for the six hours—or half day's work—began. As soon as the six hours of "turning" were accomplished, a signal was given by the "Butty-banksman," as he was called, being three loud blows by a sledge hammer on a large hollow skep, this being heard at the bottom, the word "loose all" was passed on from stage to stage until it reached the "loaders" at the coal face, when they ceased work. But as it was customary to leave the "roads" empty, the turning went on till the last truck was unloaded, thus it will be clearly seen that a half-day's work meant about nine or ten hours from the time of leaving the bank to descend to the time of returning to the same.

The men did not mind this because, as I have said, they were paid by the ton, but to the lads, who were paid by the day, what did it mean? It meant that in the winter I could only take home half a crown at the end of the week, and that after seeing nothing of the daylight the whole of the time, it being dark when we descended the pit, and dark when we came up. Sunday came round and was hailed with delight by the poor collier-lad, as on that morn he was privileged to see God's beautiful light—after gradually accustoming his eyes to bear it. The men who worked by piece-work drew money from the "Butties" weekly on account, or, as it was termed, by "subs," the settling up, or reckoning night, taking place once in two months.

RECKONING NIGHT.

The publicans, the shop-keepers, the tradesmen, the young children, the cripples, for as a rule there were a good many of these in pit villages, and the loafers were always most anxious to know when it was "reckoning night." As a rule there was no turning done on that day, and the colliers would be seen coming from the villages around attired in their best, often followed by wives, sweethearts, tradesmen, etc., for was it not "reckoning night," and if it had been a brisk time in the coal-trade, would there not be plenty of money? Wives and children needed clothes, boots, etc., and shop-keepers required their bills settled, those who had advanced money as loans demanded repayment, with interest, and the publican expected his score—and sometimes a long one—to be wiped out. The reckoning took place in the different weighing sheds and cabins on the pit-banks, and often there was much wrangling and disputing over it, ending, in some cases, in quarrels and fights. As a rule the publican got settled with first as the collier would rush off to the public-house on getting his money, the others waiting on him there to get what they could, with the result that the poor wife and children would be left to the last, and come off worst, for the others *must* be settled with, in whole or in part, or the supplies in future would be stopped.

COLLIER'S SUPPER.

Occasionally, when it was a specially good "reckoning," there would be a collier supper arranged at a public-house, when the long "club-rooms" would be prepared with tables from end to end, on which were placed huge joints of meat and vegetables all steaming hot, with pies and puddings to follow. Each collier paid half a crown for his supper and a lad one shilling, and whatever drink they consumed—which was mostly very considerable—was paid for in addition. These nights generally ended in terrible orgies, but the boys were not allowed to stay until the end. A great deal of contention and jealousy was often caused, leading to bitter quarrels and fights, and a collier fight in those days was a most repulsive scene to behold. Frequently when a dispute arose in the mine, it would be settled by a desperate fight when the disputants came to the bank, they being surrounded by those who took the different sides, and sometimes several of these would take place at the same time. Collier lads were encouraged to settle their disputes in the same fashion, and so if they continued in the mine they, as a rule, became hardened brutal miners.

It may be asked by some who read this, "Why do you give such a detailed account of your life in those early days?" My reply is, I do so for several reasons. First, because after passing through such bitter experiences and hardships in this period of my life I could never murmur or complain at my lot in after years, however sad it might be.

Second, because in after years those early experiences have been most helpful to me in my missionary work in dealing with bodies of working-men. Here is a case in point :—Many years ago I was asked to give a Gospel address to a large number of hard working-men. As I was a stranger to them, they were not disposed to listen to what I had to say. One and another seemed to think that parsons and such like men knew nothing about them, and the hardships they had to endure, etc., etc. Appeal was made to them to give me a few minutes' hearing, and if they thought then that their case was not understood I would stop. I told them that it was most likely I commenced to earn my living at an earlier period in life than any of them, had started at a lower level, and had had a fair share of struggles and hardships. These things I explained. After this they were all willing and attentive listeners. Numerous instances like the foregoing I have had in my missionary career.

Third, I place it on record, as showing the kind Providence of God, in leading me on step by step, through hardship and difficulty, trusting that it may encourage some who may be sorely pressed, to wait patiently and trust in God.

Above all, I hope that I write it for the Glory of God.

Some, however, may think my picture of hardship

and cruelty is overdrawn, and that considering the length of time since the events happened, I may have given wide scope to the imagination. If such thought, however, should be in the mind of the indulgent reader, I may say that I can remember enduring hardships, and suffering terrible cruelties, far worse than those I have referred to, in fact, indignities too bad to be recorded.

Such was the condition of things, and such were the hard times I had to pass through in this first period of my life. As I sit in my own comfortable little home, and write these words, and look back at those early days of hardship, of suffering and tears, my heart is filled with gratitude to the God of all grace, who, by His providence, has ordered my path and led me by a way that I knew not.

SECOND DECADE.

THE commencement of this period of my life found me still at work in the coal-pit. A change, however, from some cause or other, was gradually taking place in the methods used for getting out the coal. I was too young, of course, to know what was being done by "Commissions" and "Parliament," no doubt brought about by the intervention of Lord Ashley. This one thing, however, I had good reason to know, that the hard cruel lot of the poor collier lad was being mitigated.

It had been decided to have ponies in the pits, but it took a long time to prepare the main roads for this, as the coal seam was only between three and four feet in thickness, and the height of the roads had to be increased. In due course all was ready, and the ponies were let down into the mine. I was associated with the man who looked after the welfare of the pretty little animals, and as he was most kind and attentive to them, I suppose he was led instinctively to be more kind to the collier lad. Many of the boys, as well as some of the men, had to find work in other fields, but I was kept on. My lot was never so hard afterwards, and I had various employments, none of which however could be termed congenial in those dismal mines.

I had some very providential escapes from accidents and death. One day the roof of a part of the road where I was working with a pony appeared likely to fall. A "butty" was watching it, and said it would be all right till the turning was done. On going under some little while after, however, it fell just as the pony with a train of trucks was passing, but the mass fell on several trucks behind the first one on which I was sitting, and so I escaped.

THIRSTING FOR KNOWLEDGE.

Not being so jaded or worn down by slavery as under the former state of things, I was now anxious to improve my mind. I was encouraged and assisted in this by the vicar and the private tutor to his family, and most week evenings I was in the tutor's room receiving lessons. He was also my Sunday School teacher, and as he was a godly man, I derived from him and the vicar good knowledge of the Scriptures. I little thought at that time when my mind was being stored with God's Word (for I was accustomed to repeat whole chapters, yes, and almost whole books of Holy Writ on Sabbath evenings at the Vicarage, and other places) how God was preparing me for future service. I was very regular and attentive both at Sunday School and Church, and having a pretty good voice, was one of the principal singers. My friends also lent me helpful books which I read and studied eagerly in my spare time, and for which in after years I often felt thankful.

ANOTHER CRISIS.

My physical infirmity—before referred to—increased so very painfully that it was with difficulty I could continue to work in the mine. The crisis came at last. I had been working on the Saturday, and the next day, Sunday, being the Church Anniversary, I was to take a leading part in the little choir. I went to bed, but the pain was so intense that I could not sleep. Towards morning the tumour burst and I was rendered unconscious. For some days I lay in that state, with the tumour continually discharging, while the doctor said that there was not the least hope for my recovery. After some time, however, the bleeding stopped, and ultimately I regained consciousness, and gradually recovered. Weakened in body, I was a long time regaining strength. I was kindly cared for by some friends, including the vicar and his wife, by whom under God I was brought back to life. In this mysterious manner did God interpose and deliver me from the pit, for I never went to work in the mine again, but my path was turned another way.

It was thought by many that I should never be able to work again, and now the question was, what would become of me. It was evident also that my mother was wearing herself out with her hard lot, and the heavy grief she had to bear. Whether it was through these or other causes I know not, but there was manifested such a general sympathy with us from all quarters, that my mother had more orders for work, and of a better kind, while friends on every hand seemed to be raised up to aid us.

As I got stronger I was able to do light work, and so earned a little, while at the same time I received further education at the vicarage.

About this time some railway work commenced and this brought a number of workmen into the villages. Some of the men on the works were earnest Christians, but the bulk of them were very dissipated, and I remember how the former used to meet for special prayer on behalf of the latter.

Special religious meetings were held in the fields and buildings and quite a revival of religion broke out in several of the villages—including the one in which I lived. I used to attend some of the meetings, and I well remember how my young heart throbbed as I listened to men telling of their new-found joy and love for the Saviour. For a time I was under deep and serious impressions, but some old professors threw cold water upon these impressions saying that I was too young, and when I got older I should be able to understand things better.

One thing that gave me pleasure was reading the Bible to groups of men during their mealtimes and of an evening. Only a few of the men who had been awakened and converted could read, and so I was asked by those who could not read to relate to them stories from both the Old and New Testaments. I recall how these hardy sons of toil would listen with rapt attention

READING TO CONVERTED NAVVIES.

and would even weep while I read to them from the Book of books, or related to them some of its thrilling stories.

A FURTHER CRISIS.

About this time it could be clearly seen that my poor mother's health was fast failing, and at length she had to give up the struggle, and calling me to her side, she told me to be a good lad, to remember the instruction I had received, to read my Bible and pray to God to guide me to Jesus and meet her in heaven. The end came more rapidly than was expected, for the dropsy from which she suffered increased so quickly that it soon reached the heart, and so one day the sad news was announced that my mother was dead. That day can never be forgotten. I went into the garden and cried till I thought my heart would break. We laid her to rest in the churchyard, near the graves where her ancestors slept. That night my little brother and I wept together a great deal in bed, in the little cottage where we were born, and felt that another crisis had come, the result of which it was impossible to foresee.

From that time my wanderings began.

I had to leave the village, having obtained a situation with a man who resided in a place on the edge of the forest, and who carried out all the iron-working at the pits where I formerly worked. It was quite three miles from his house to the pits, but I was not sent every day. Sometimes I was driven over in a cart, but mostly I had to walk. As I lived in the house, I had better food and so grew stronger, while, in the work of constructing the various machines, rail trucks, etc., I became very useful. I might very probably have been apprenticed to my master, but that required a premium, and I had no friend to find the money.

In the course of time I left there, as I wanted higher wages and these I could not obtain. In the providence of God my lot was cast in various places, sometimes in association with good men, and at other times with bad men. I am thankful to God, as I look back over those years, that the early Christian influences which I received from my good friends always had the effect of keeping me back from open and flagrant sins into which I saw many young people plunging.

I need not follow my wanderings for some years, as my life at this time was of the ordinary kind, further than to say that before I was nineteen I was a strong square-built young man, at which age my wanderings brought me to London. Sir Joseph Paxton was then erecting the Crystal Palace and it was while working there that he undertook to raise a corps of working men to go out to the Crimean War.

THIRD DECADE.

ABOUT this time I entered upon what was perhaps the most eventful period of my life. Being strong, and active, with a remarkable spirit of daring, intense love of adventure, spoken of as genial, fairly glib in speech, reading and singing tolerably well, these qualities, wherever I went, seemed to draw around me numbers of compeers, who were perhaps not so well furnished. Then I looked much older than I was, having a black beard and a strong manly appearance which classed me, though young, with men much older.

THE CRIMEAN WAR.

I witnessed numbers of soldiers assembling in different parts of London, who were being dispatched to the war, and as I read of the terrible sufferings and carnage among our poor fellows my young ardent spirit was stirred within me. In later years there have been opportunities of witnessing far larger numbers of troops, departing for a more distant seat of war, and in much larger vessels than those of fifty years ago.

When Sir Joseph Paxton started to raise a corps of one thousand, or more, strong, working men, by order of the government, to go out to the Crimea and make roads, erect huts, or to perform any kind of work other then carrying arms and fighting, I was only too eager to offer myself. I had grave doubts as to my being up to the standard, remembering my early affliction, but when I had gone through the ordeal and was certified to be "sound in wind and limb," I felt equal to anything.

When this "Army Works Corps"—as it was called—was formed I was selected to take charge of a company of these sturdy, hardworking, in many cases hard-drinking, and hard-headed fellows. The men worked in their various companies or gangs at the Crystal Palace until the ship was ready for their embarkation. It was at this time that that very excellent lady, and good friend of the working man, Miss Marsh, used to visit the men at work at the Crystal Palace grounds, giving earnest and faithful addresses and distributing Christian literature and Scripture portions among us. Every man as he left to embark for the East received a copy of Holy Scripture from her hands, and I have reason to know that some of them never forgot her warm shake of the hand, or the tearful look of her eyes, as she besought them, one and all, to look to the Lord Jesus, and bade them good-bye. I do not know if Miss Marsh ever saw many, or even any, of them again, but I had the great pleasure of meeting her a few years since, and although she had become blind, and therefore could not see me, she expressed her joy at the opportunity of having a talk with me.

The steamship *Azoff*, which was to take about five hundred of us to the front, was berthed in the Thames, and when we, with our equipments, were all aboard, away she sailed. Our voyage out was a long chapter of accidents, and it was no light task to control such turbulent spirits, although we were under martial law. There was an abundance of strong drink on board, and as the men, being in receipt of good wages, had plenty of money, and plenty of time on their hands, they spent both in gambling, drinking, etc.

The voyage was a stormy one for the most part, and while crossing the Bay of Biscay our engines broke down, and the vessel began to drift with a strong current into danger. All the men had to get below to their berths by 9.30, and at 10 o'clock lights were put out; but on one terribly rough night, when there was a fear that our disabled vessel would founder, it was with difficulty that I got some of my men below, as they said they saw great danger. At length we succeeded, and were able to turn in, but soon after we heard a cry on deck, "A man overboard." A line was thrown out, with a lifebuoy attached to it, but in the darkness and raging sea of that awful night nothing could be seen or heard. I found that it was one of the men of my company, and his mate said that he could not keep him below. He had rushed up on deck, undressed, and, seizing a lifebuoy, had jumped overboard before his mates could stop him. Poor J. S—— was the first man we lost; he was a finely built man, and had been accustomed to the sea, but he told his companions that he had never been in such a tempest, and he saw fear.

I had known him for some time before he joined the Corps, but he was always a dissipated man, and, no doubt, was in drink when he took his fatal " leap in the dark."

We managed to reach Gibraltar, and, when repairs were completed, our ship started for Malta, where we hoped to arrive in good time, but she was destined to further disaster. After about two days' fast steaming it was rumoured that we were " out of our right course," but we went driving ahead.

On a fine calm evening, if anyone had walked along the deck with an observant eye, he would have seen a group of men in one part dancing to the tune of a fiddle, in another part men playing cards and gambling, others discussing the problems of the war, but he would have seen the greater number drinking, smoking, and singing love and war songs. All the men were got below, with the usual difficulty, at the proper time. Now, I have often thought of the scene on deck that evening, and have, since my conversion to God, referred to it as follows. Suppose any man on that evening had stood amidship, and raising his hand, had called the men to a prayer meeting and had commenced by himself offering a prayer to God. Well, I don't hesitate to say that there were men on deck who would have thought no more of throwing him overboard than they did the empty barrels from which they had drunk all the beer. But before many hours had passed, what a change took place.

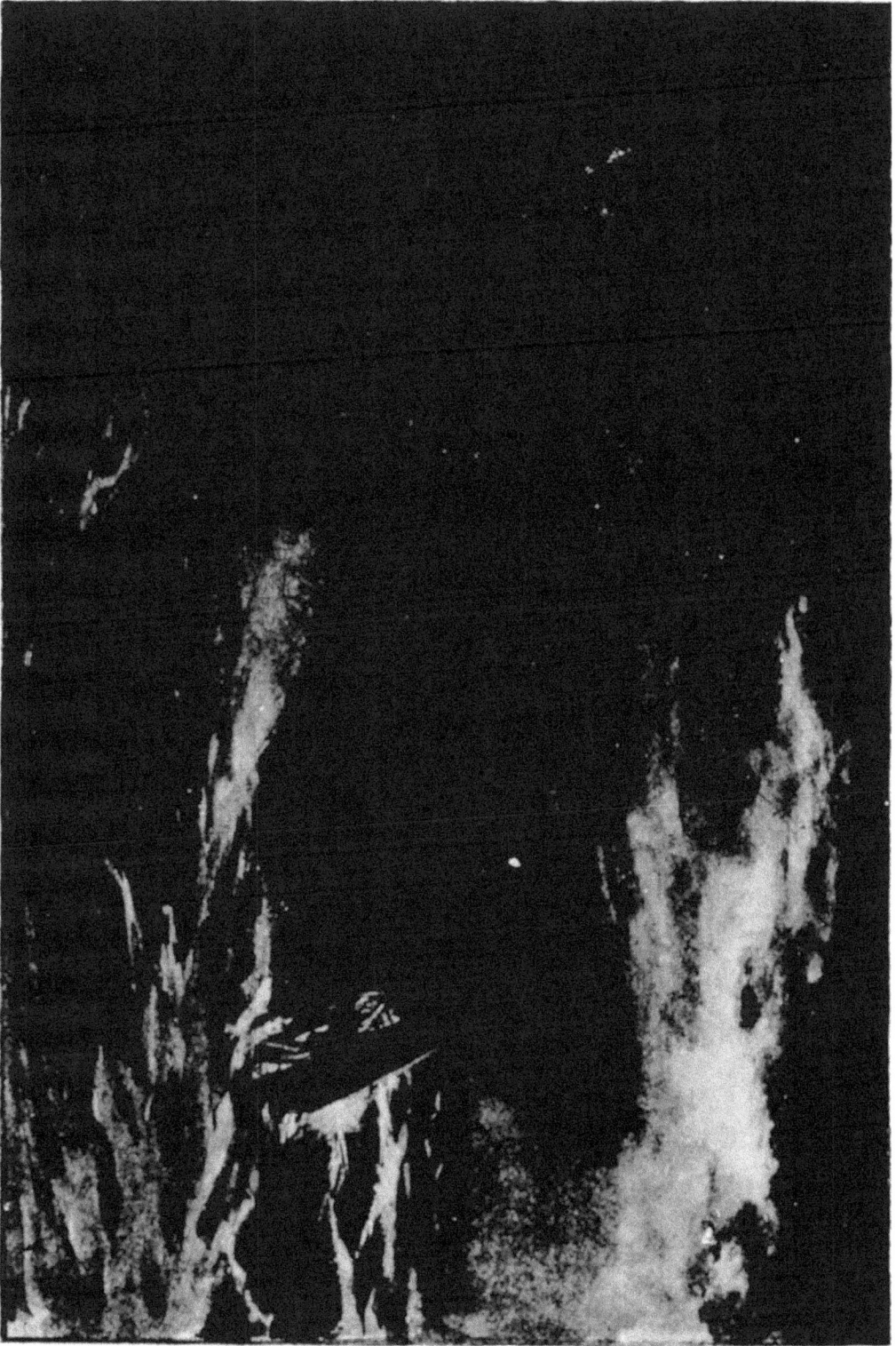

"IN TEN MINUTES WE SHALL BE AT THE BOTTOM!"

A SUDDEN ALARM.

About one o'clock, when most, if not all, of the men were asleep in their bunks, and the steamer was forging ahead at full speed, a tremendous shock was experienced, by which nearly every man was thrown out of his berth, and before we had time to consider a second bump was felt which seemed to make the ship quiver from stem to stern. A rushing about on deck, shouting out of orders, stopping of engines, and cries to each other of half-naked men as they clambered on deck, plainly indicated that something terrible had happened. The doctor, who slept near me, said it was a collision, and so, hastily putting on some clothing I went up on deck, and I have often described the sight I then beheld.

There stood the captain, calm, but prepared for the worst. As soon as the ship's carpenter ran to his side, and told him what he had found out, he raised his hands and exclaimed, "In ten minutes we shall be at the bottom." Now, behold the change from the previous evening. What a prayer meeting, or, rather, what cries in prayer from all parts of the ship. Yes, the thought of only a short time to live, of being so near to death and eternity, impelled most of us to cry spontaneously to God to help and save. The captain, and officers, had put on lifebelts, for the vessel seemed about to founder, and by my side stood the pay-master—a Dutchman—with a belt round his waist full of money. The chief officer asked him, "What have you there?"

and he stammered out "Mein money." "Throw it away," said the officer, "that will sink you; and put on this lifebelt." The belt of money was thrown away, and the lifebelt took its place, and I have often thought since how true what Satan said—though not true of Job—"All that a man hath, will he give for his life." The boats were crowded with men, and it was a wonder that they were not lowered, in which event numbers of men would have been lost. The ship was evidently across a sunken reef, for the captain was afraid she would break up amidships. A rather heavy swell was on, and all at once she seemed to heave up. Then she plunged stem first into the sea, and oh! the consternation that then seized everyone. As her head went under the sea, and kept there, about one-fourth part of the ship being under water, while the stern was out of the water, everyone thought she must go down.

After a short period of intense anxiety, a shout was heard, "She floats," and it was then found that her "bulkheads" had not given way, and as she was divided into five water-tight compartments, by these the water was only in the first one, which, however, kept her head under.

Now began the struggle for life—as we believed it to be—and the command was given for every man to work with all his might at the pumps, and in lightening the fore part of the ship by throwing cargo overboard. All set to work in real earnest, stimulated by the promise that if the ship could be worked to the nearest port we should have another vessel to take us onward. The pumping had no effect, for the water could not be reduced at all, but after throwing a considerable part of the cargo overboard, or removing it to the after part of the ship, at which the men worked for two days and nights without ceasing, the stern was brought down so that the " propellers " could work. It was decided to steer the ship for Tunis, that being the nearest port we could make, and with care and difficulty this was done. As we steamed slowly up the Bay, taking soundings all the way, the ship was at length brought up, and all hearts seemed to beat lighter at the thought of being out of this great peril of the deep. I now was told that our vessel had gone very much out of her course through coming in contact with other iron ships at Gibraltar, which had affected our magnet, and that the reef we had struck was called the " Skerka," that it was most dangerous, being ten feet or more under water. We were told that a ship foundered on it some years before with four hundred troops on board.

In the course of a few hours some high officials of the port came aboard, including the " Bey," and the English Consul. It was then found that the ship could not be repaired there, neither could another vessel be provided to take off the men. Upon examination it was found that there was a terrible opening under her bows, besides other damages caused by the tremendous concussion on that fearful night. However, blankets and sailcloths were drawn under the damaged place, and, the ship's carpenter pronouncing her seaworthy, it was decided to take her to Malta.

At this, there was manifested great discontent among the men, and the " Bey " and Consul asked that their representatives should state what they desired. As I was first on the list, I had to state my case. I related how the Captain had encouraged the men to work night and day, with but little rest and food, by assuring them that if the ship could be kept afloat, and got into port, another vessel would be provided to take them onward; that we had done the best we could so far, but were not prepared to run further risks in her. Others spoke in the same strain, and some much stronger. The " Bey " said, if we refused to go in her to Malta, we must go on shore and be put in prison till a vessel called to take us back to England, there to be punished as our Government decided. After a further consultation with the Captain, the officials decided to muster the men on deck, and take a division of those who were willing to go, and those who were unwilling, the " ayes " filing to one end of the ship, the " noes " to the other end. Again, as our company was first on the rota, I had to lead, and passed on to the place of the " noes," and everyone of the men of whom I had charge followed, with one exception. The majority of the others went the other way. The Consul expressed himself as being pleased at the way the men had behaved all through this perilous affair, and that there had been no sign of insubordination. He would, therefore, find another vessel to take those to Malta who were unwilling to go in the steamer. So ended this somewhat painful ordeal, but I had to pay for it when the war was over, and I returned home.

LEAVING TUNIS.

As soon as a little sailing ship could be got ready we were put on board, and immediately the steamer left for Malta—a distance of about 300 miles. When the wind freshened, for the weather had become very calm, our little craft also set sail. We reached Malta safely, the steamer arriving there some time before us, but she had to steam slowly, the fore part being so low in the water. When she was got into dock and examined both officers and crew said that, had they known the extent of the damage she had sustained, they would have been afraid to navigate her to Malta. They had "to thank their lucky stars," they added, for a smooth passage, for had it been rough it would have been most perilous.

MALTA.

Our men were quartered on a part of the island called "Lazeretto," in huts, etc., which were used for isolation in time of infectious diseases. It was a point of rocky land, opposite Valetta, and reached by crossing a wide bay. Here we had to remain for some weeks while the steamer was being repaired and got ready for sea again. We had a strange and difficult experience while here, for in the first place, all our provisions had to be brought across the bay to us and sometimes the men had to go short; then it was impossible to keep the men from going across to the town where they gave way to drink, and got into all kinds of trouble. The natives would rob the men, and buy the very clothes off their backs, while in a state of intoxication. So serious did this condition of things become, that many of the men lost the greater part of their "kit," and we had to represent this to the Governor of the island, who sent some policemen to search the dealers' shops, when most of the clothing was recovered, the natives having to bear the whole loss. While lying here, a fine young fellow belonging to my company disappeared. It was supposed that he walked into the Bay one night when in drink, and was drowned. It was several days before we knew what had become of him, and then his body was discovered by some young natives as they were diving for coins, etc. They brought up his body, and we buried it.

AFLOAT AGAIN.

The men were glad when they embarked again and steamed away from Malta. All hoped that the remainder of the voyage would be more propitious than the former part had been, as they were most anxious to be at the seat of war.

At the entrance of the "Dardanelles" were a number of sailing vessels waiting for a fair wind to take them up, for the current here is very strong. In those days all kinds of vessels were engaged in conveying material, etc., for the war, but now, as is generally known, the Government can subsidize any number of fine ocean-going steamers, as they did during the war in South Africa.

Constantinople was safely reached, and we remained there about 36 hours. The port was crowded with vessels, some carrying material to the front, others returning from the seat of war. On the other side of the Bay was " Scutari," where were the hospitals, composed of wooden huts and tents, to which the sick and wounded—or, at least, some of them—were brought from the front. It was here that Miss Florence Nightingale—that noble pioneer of nurses—was struggling along with a handful of willing helpers, amongst a mass of diseased and mangled soldiers, many of whom, when they came under her charge, were, to all appearances, more dead than alive.

The hour for leaving Constantinople had come, and the men having been hurried on board, the moorings were cast off, and the ship's head was turned towards the Bosphorus. The vessel had scarcely got under weigh before it was discovered that several men were left on shore. They were hurried off in a boat, and when they were aboard we steamed away. The next day one of these men, a strong well-built fellow, was very ill, and the doctor, after examining him, pronounced him to be in a dying state. He had evidently contracted some fatal malady while on shore, and all efforts to save his life were unavailing. In a few hours he died.

This was the third man we had lost since leaving England, and he, too, belonged to my company.

A BURIAL AT SEA.

A burial at sea is a most solemn scene to those at least who are witnessing it for the first time. I am not equal to a graphic description of the scene, but for the sake of those who have not been present at such a ceremony, I will simply describe what took place, as it fell to my lot again—the man being under my charge—to carry out the proceedings. As soon as the poor fellow was dead, preparations were begun for the burial. Two fire-bars were placed on either side of the lower part of the corpse, and it was bound up in blankets, etc., and brought on deck. The men assembled around, and for once you could see them calm, and for the most part in a thoughtful mood, for there, on one of the "hatches," one end of which rested on the bulwark on the leeward side of the ship, while the other end rested on a support somewhat higher than the bulwark, lay the mortal remains of a comrade, who was yesterday as gay as any of them. The service for the burial of the dead at sea was read, while the men stood with uncovered heads; the sea was fairly calm, so that the words could be heard by those gathered round, and when the passage was read, "We therefore commit his body to the deep," the upper end of the "hatch" was lifted, and the remains of this young man slid down into the waters of the Black Sea. For a moment I' watched the rapid descent into the deep, and then there flashed across my mind what I had been taught in my childhood days of the great resurrection morn, when the sea shall give up its dead. The management of the ship went on as usual, and everyone soon fell back into his old method of careless living.

The next day, towards evening, we were sailing straight for Balaklava Harbour, when an English gunboat bore down toward us and signalled to us to heave-to, as there was no room for any more vessels in the harbour. Our Captain paid no heed, but kept steaming ahead, when a shot from the gunboat came across our bows, and as we kept steaming, a second one came nearer to us. Our Captain signalled that he had starving men aboard, and he should run the ship into the harbour unless prevented doing so by her being sunk.

THE THEATRE OF WAR.

The great war has long since passed into history, with the tremendous sacrifice to five nations of men and money. I shall therefore only refer to those events of which I had experience, or with which I was intimately associated.

The morning after the events recorded in the previous section we landed and began to prepare our encampment on the slope of some rising ground about two miles from the harbour. Tents, huts, and all kinds of stores, etc., were brought up from the ship, and in a few days we had our rude quarters ready. We were employed for some time making roads and erecting "huts" for regiments coming out and for some regiments which had lost numbers of men through being under canvas.

ROUGHING IT.

It was a trying experience for some time to myself and the men with me, as the weather was very stormy. One night a terrible gale swept down the hillside, and the tent under which I was *trying* to sleep was carried clean away, whilst the torrent of water rushing down the slope washed the ground clear of everything movable. In the darkness I scrambled up at the first shock, and, seizing a little bag that was under my head, in which were a few important and necessary things for campaigning, and the Bible given to me by Miss Marsh, I groped my way to an officer's hut, where I was readily received, and given dry things, for I had nothing on but under garments, and they were drenched.

A CRIMEAN WINTER.

A large number of men had perished the previous winter through being under canvas, not always by frost, although many succumbed to that, but by the men closing the tent all round, so as to prevent the cold getting in, and putting the little charcoal fire in the centre, then lying down to sleep, with their feet towards the

A STORM IN THE CRIMEA.

fire. This to many proved the sleep of death. In spite of the printed cautions against acting in so foolish a manner, many did it, and, therefore, the authorities determined to have as many wooden huts as possible before the next cold season came in. It was our work to hurry this along with all possible speed, yet one sad event must be mentioned here. We usually built the huts in rows of eight or ten joined together. One such row was erected on the slope of a hill, a short distance from Balaclava. The roof was covered with felt well soaked with tar, and the first night it was occupied by troops just landed from a troop-ship, and after many of them had become senseless through spirit-drinking, the place caught fire, and the flames ran from end to end so rapidly that the whole structure was quickly consumed. Some escaped being more or less severely burnt, but others, alas, perished in the terribly rapid conflagration, which consumed them entirely, the tremendous heat, intensified by the burning tar, melting watches and money found on them.

Commodious huts were erected at certain distances from each other, on the principal road from Balaclava to Sebastopol, or to within a gunshot distance from the latter place. These were used as a sort of ambulance station, where good fires were kept burning, and stores for drugs and spirits which were used as restoratives on those who had been overcome by the cold. Several of the largest ones were used as temporary hospitals, where doctors were in readiness to perform surgical operations, which were very frequent by day and night during the severe winter of 1855-6. This road was thronged by troops and "fatigue parties," who were conveying all kinds of stores, etc., from Balaclava to the front, Balaclava being the principal, or about this time the only place for landing commodities necessary for carrying on the war; and while some things were carried by a single line railway, for a few miles, the greater number were conveyed in carts, waggons, or mule-packs, along this well-made (for this country at least) "macadamised" road.

It is not easy to describe the severity of a Russian winter, and its terrible effects on the thousands of poor fellows who were so ill-prepared to withstand it. Among the thousands who passed to and fro along this road, numbers were frost bitten, and it was a frequent occurrence to see men removed from the horses or waggons and taken into these wayside huts to be dealt with. The amputation of toes or fingers, and sometimes of a foot or leg was necessary, in order to save life, and I have known cases of men being removed from the saddle, dead through the intense cold. There were special men set apart to ride up and down the road, to look out for thieves or spies, to stop any suspicious looking person, and also to have any who were frost bitten removed to the huts. Sometimes a team would be stopped by one of these men, and he would order a man—whom he had noticed—to be lifted down, when it would be found that the poor fellow was dead.

FATAL DELUSIONS.

There were two fatal delusions which possessed thousands of men, as to how best to preserve themselves from the sad effects of the severe frost and cold. One was the fatal practice previously referred to of tightly closing the tent at night, and placing a charcoal fire in the centre; the other was the drinking of ardent spirits—such as rum, brandy, or Russian fiery spirit—most of it being of the worst kind, stupefying deadly stuff. I have no hesitation in saying that these two things, and the terrible scourge of cholera in the hot seasons, claimed far more precious lives than the sword, or the engines of war in actual conflict. The drink delusion appeared to have such a fascinating power over men that although they saw its fearful effects all around by day and also by night, they seemed powerless to resist it. Let me illustrate my point. On the main road I have been describing, when the traffic stopped at " sun-down "—as soon as the latter event took place it became dark, there being no twilight—parties of men were appointed to patrol the road, to search for those who were overcome by the cold, or lying down asleep, or frost-bitten. These would be carried into the huts and efforts made to restore them before the fires and by drugs and rubbing. Some would succumb and such would mostly be from among those who were found asleep by the roadside. Now, it was often found that these, on starting out, had taken a good glass of " grog," as they called it, to keep them warm and keep the cold out. After a while the feeling of drowsiness overcame them, and if they were not run along by others, or got to a warm place they would lie down and unconsciously go to sleep, sometimes never to awake. Now the delusion was in this, that some of those who were out on duty, say the previous night, or a few nights before, bringing men in and trying to reanimate them, would themselves be found in that dreadful position, say, to-night, which would perhaps cost them their life, or the loss of a limb, or they might just escape.

DRINK.

With many the awful craving for strong drink was insatiable : they would expend all their own earnings on the deadly stuff and some would rob their comrades, whilst I have even known sick ones to be murdered to get the money from under the pillow or bed for drink. I have witnessed some painful cases of punishments inflicted on men who have been caught red handed, as it were, in terrible crimes. Of course all were tried by " court-martial," for everyone was under martial law, and our corps, although they could not be compelled to carry arms, and fight, were nevertheless subject to the same law. Every day witnessed men undergoing all kinds of punishment for crimes of which drink was the cause. A man detected in committing a crime was court-martialled on the spot, sentenced and punished at once.

One painful case I will just note. It was that of a

man in our corps; a fine, strong fellow, a quarryman from the West of England. He had given way to drink to an alarming extent—maddened with it—and in order to get it, he had robbed several men of considerable sums of money. He was tried and sentenced to receive the next morning, five dozen lashes with the "cat-o'-nine-tails." The Provost Marshal decided that this should be an exemplary punishment, as this kind of crime appeared to be very frequent.

THE DEGRADING "CAT."

To witness this degrading scene was my painful duty, and so when it was light all our men who were in that locality, with a number of troops, were mustered at the bugle-blast to see the punishment inflicted. A hollow square was formed, a heavy cart brought into the centre, tilted up, with the shafts in the air; the Provost Marshal rode on to the field and stood beside a big drum turned on end. The prisoner was marched to the place of punishment by an escort, and the men called to "attention." An officer then read aloud the prisoner's crime, and the sentence passed upon him, when amidst a deep silence the poor fellow was stripped to his loins, and tied up to the side of the cart. Two stalwart drummers took off their coats, etc., and rolling up the sleeves of their under vests, took the "cat" out of their respective cases and having drawn the "nine tails"—or leather thongs—between their fingers, with a curious flourish of the "cat" over head each time, they stood ready to discharge their painful task. The officer in charge commanded the men how to inflict the punishment. Each man was to give twelve stripes, alternately, one being a right-handed and the other a left-handed man, " and now," he added, " do your duty."

The prisoner submitted to every detail of preparation, evidently determined to take his punishment " like a man," and it must be said a finer specimen of physical perfection it would have been difficult to find. I stood near our chief officer and the doctor to behold this ordeal, and I shall never forget the impression it made on me, and also on many others who were present. The right-handed man commenced the flogging, and as the heavy thuds of the nine thongs fell on the poor man's back, one could see the flesh and muscles quiver at every stroke, the stripes falling at an angle of forty-five degrees from the right shoulder. At the end of the first twelve strokes the left-handed man began, the thongs from his " cat " falling diagonally across the former. I cannot describe the condition of the poor man's back when the second twelve stripes were ended, suffice it to say, that painful in the extreme though it must have been, the man never said a word or uttered the exclamation " Oh ! " While the third dozen strokes were being given, both the chief officer and doctor became alarmed at the apparent stolidity of the man, and so the latter went to the side of the poor fellow to watch his features. Just before the end of this part of the punishment was reached the man seized the rim of the cart wheel between his teeth, and his face was turning black when the doctor held up his hand. The flogging ceased, the man was unloosed, and he fell to the ground insensible. After the doctor had administered a restorative, he revived and was able to sit up again. His lacerated back was dressed, and after his clothes were put on, he was able to stand. Our chief officer—who was also a civilian—was deeply moved, and addressing the poor man in a sympathetic tone said, " I am very sorry to have to see you undergo such punishment for wrong doing, and I hope you will try and be a better man. Anyhow "—and here he took him by the hand—" you can be assured that, as long as I have command of this corps, whether you are a better man or not, neither you nor any one else under me shall undergo such a degrading ordeal as this one." The tears rushed from the poor fellow's eyes and he simply uttered, " I'll try." The man kept his word for he was sober and industrious to the end of our stay.

Now I firmly believe that it was not the brutal punishment that softened and subdued the man, but the kind sympathetic words of the chief officer.

UNDER FIRE.

I have already said that, as we were not soldiers, we could not be compelled to carry arms and fight, neither could we be compelled to work under fire. Our chief officer was asked if any of his men would volunteer to go into Sebastopol to assist in certain work there and in the surrounding forts. The whole of our company offered themselves with the exception of one man who was in hospital, so the next morning we entered the town under cover of the darkness, and found quarters in a large warehouse alongside the entrance of the docks.

Our first night in this place was a strange experience, as none of us had ever been in such a position before. A desultory firing from the Russians kept us awake the whole night, with an occasional shot crashing into the buildings in the town, or a shell exploding near us. After a few nights, however, we became accustomed to this state of things, and could sleep soundly. One of our men could not settle down to this new order, neither could he sleep. He was a married man with wife and children at home, and as we were afraid he would lose his reason he was sent back to the rear.

Our work was to assist the " sappers and miners "— as they were then called—in taking machinery to pieces and sending it away, getting guns and valuable timber out of the town and fortifications, mining and blowing up the docks and principal buildings in the town, and, in fact, to remove and send away anything that was of value and could be removed, and destroy the rest. Many of the most valuable guns, including a whole " field train," were run into the harbour—near the sides of the dock quays and other places—before the Russians evacuated this side of the town, passing over to the north side on pontoon bridges, which they destroyed when their troops were all over. The Redán and the Malakhoff were two hills a short distance from the wall of the town, and out of these two fortifications we got some guns and some " lignum-vitæ " timber, which was very valuable.

I had some narrow escapes while working in and around this place.

One day while our men were at work in a " bomb-proof " part of the Redan, several officers were talking with me outside the fort, when a shot struck the rock close to their feet and ricochetted for a considerable distance. We saw the mark it had made on striking the rock, and smelt the fire it caused, but the only remark made was, " We must separate from one another a little." There was a deal of firing at times from the Russians' lines. Their front extended along the north side of the harbour, and for several miles inland along the bank of the River Tchernaya, which flowed into the harbour; but our guns never returned the fire, as I was told that every shot fired by the English cost the country £40. During the eleven months' siege of Sebastopol, before it was evacuated—for it was not taken by the allied forces—there was a determined attack on the French and the Sardinians in the Tchernaya Valley, a few miles from the town, where the river was narrow. On the 16th August, 1855, Prince Gortschakoff hurled 50,000 troops on a few regiments who were protecting this part, and it was thought an attempt would be made to get behind the besiegers that way. It was, however, repulsed with heavy losses, the enemy leaving over 3,300 slain, 1,650 wounded, and 600 were taken prisoners! The loss of the allies was 1,200, and the victory appeared to be mainly due to the gallantry of the Sardinians.

The assault on the Redan and Malakhoff was made on the 8th of the next month, September, and that night the Russians left the town, destroying all they could and sinking or burning the greater part of their fleet in the harbour. The Emperor Nicholas died the previous March, and his son, Alexander, became Czar, and although he was a far more humane man there was no change of policy. I just refer to this in order that my readers may consider that if such awful destruction of precious lives and property could be accomplished in those days, what frightful loss—beyond conception— must take place when contending nations confront each other with the diabolical engines of war in these days! Surely all lovers of the human family must desire that the Peace Conferences now being held, may tend to dispose civilized nations to settle disputes by arbitration instead of war. "Give peace in our time, O Lord," should be the earnest prayer of all followers of the Prince of Peace.

SEBASTOPOL.

To resume the narrative of my doings in this place, I may say that there was much valuable property and stores of various kinds in the town, and what could not be sent away we sought to destroy. The worst days for us were those when companies of soldiers came from the camp to the town to pull timber out of the houses to carry away for fuel, or when crews of merchant ships came to look at the place and to carry away with them mementoes of the town. On such occasions the firing was rather hot, and sometimes we had to get under cover—as there were many bomb-proof places in the town. Our provisions used to be brought to us every day from camp by a pair of strong mules and waggon, and one day when some brisk firing from the north side was giving us some trouble, having unloaded our provisions under cover, our transport-driver had to dash up a steep ascent, through a gateway in the wall, and so get under cover on the outer side. This steep bit of road was exposed to the view of the " star " fort on the north side, and it was often raked by their fire, and on this occasion no sooner had the waggon got through to the other side of the wall, than several round shots came flying up the road ; one, however, pierced the soft stone wall and struck one of the mule's head off, bespattering with blood the driver, who was riding on the other one. (I may say that this wall was perforated with round shot holes as though they had been bored.) The shock was such that the poor fellow could not bring our provision the next day, and so we had to send men to camp for it.

A LOST MEAL.

As a rule there was more firing from the north side on Sunday than on a week-day. I believe it was because so many persons came from the rear and the ships to see the place. A company of "artificers" were sent from a "man-of-war" to assist in taking to pieces some valuable engines. The men were quartered in the large warehouse with us; the officer elected to quarter himself in a workshop in an exposed position, near to their work. On the first Sunday morning that they were in the town, he asked me if we worked on Sundays, and when I said we did not, he replied, "Well, *we* shall, for we cannot waste a day." His "orderly" prepared him a breakfast about 10 o'clock—for it was winter—and his men started work, but he had scarcely begun his meal when visitors to the town were seen coming down the slopes, and the firing began. He was in the act of drinking a cup of warm coffee when a shot went through the place, carrying away his improvised table and the whole of its contents, but the officer was unhurt. He coolly told his servant to rig him up another breakfast, and he just had it on the other side of the shop, but the firing was too hot for his men to continue work, and, therefore, they had to rest on Sunday. The officer would not leave his quarters for a "bomb-proof," but remained there till their job was finished. Such was the spirit of daring.

SEVERAL NARROW ESCAPES.

If any of our men were outside the town at the time of the night guard going on duty, I had to report it at the Commandant's quarters, so that the absentees would be allowed to enter the town, if they presented themselves.

One very stormy night I was finding my way to report to the official about 9 o'clock, and passing a very dark corner I was challenged by a sentinel, who was in a sheltered place. I did not hear and so kept feeling my way along until I heard the sharp click of the rifle and at once called out. The soldier said he saw my figure on the ridge, and challenged me twice, and he was going to fire just as I answered.

On another occasion we were getting some logs of valuable timber out of the Redan down the hill-side into the road, where an arm of the harbour ran up the valley, beyond the end of which, for some distance, was an extensive marshy bog. There were other people moving about that day besides us who were at work here, and the enemy kept up a desultory fire. Several shells were sent up from their mortars, some fell short of where we were and one or two went beyond. At length, I suppose, they judged our distance fairly well, for we could hear one coming down near to us. Some ran for cover, but I was out in the open valley and could only lie down. The deadly missile fell in the bog some yards from me and exploded. It made a

E

tremendous pit—for it fell deep in the mud—but besides being perhaps a little bespattered with the latter, I escaped unhurt.

A DANGEROUS FREAK.

Among the many reckless things that I was associated with in this place, perhaps the following was the most daring. About every week, and sometimes several times a week, a flag of truce was hoisted, either on our side or on the Russians'. If this was responded to, hostilities ceased, and if despatches were to pass from one side to the other, or from both sides, such as negotiations for exchange of prisoners, etc., then a boat would start from either side, and they would meet about half way across the harbour—the whole distance was about one mile. A large vessel sunk near the middle had a mast standing above the water; at this spot the boats met, and if one was there first it would wait for the other to come. Here negotiations would be carried on by responsible officers or despatches handed over. While the white flag was flying on the Russian Fort, any number of persons could assemble anywhere in the fire-zone with safety, but as soon as they hauled down their flag, they would open fire. I have known them do this sometimes before our boat had reached home, and, of course, before our flag was lowered, but as we have already said, at this time our artillery never returned the fire. Now our boat was an old battered one, and very leaky, and the coxswain was most anxious to obtain a better one. Four oarsmen

A DANGEROUS FREAK.

and the coxswain manned the boat when it carried a flag-of-truce, and sometimes two officers, one of whom could interpret, if necessary, accompanied them. The coxswain, with whom I was very familiar, had often seen a good boat, about the size of ours, lying alongside a vessel in the enemy's waters, and felt he would like to secure it.

One day our flag-of-truce boat had to wait some time at the place of meeting for the Russian boat, and while so waiting he took the bearings of his coveted prize, as to how it lay and was fastened—for he could see everything plainly from where he was—and he made up his mind to obtain it, if he could get volunteers to assist him. In the evening he asked me to make one of four oarsmen to go with him on this rather risky expedition. Three other reliable men being found, and all pledged to secrecy, whatever might happen, we got the old boat ready, muffled the oars, and each of us having instructions from the coxswain how to act by his sign, for not a word was to be uttered, we waited for his time to start, as we had implicit trust in him.

When it was sufficiently dark, we went to the little cove where the boat lay, and took our places ready to start. Now, no one but ourselves knew of this freak, not even the men who were usually at the oars, when she carried the flag-of-truce, as the coxswain said it would be best for them to know nothing about it, as no one could tell what might happen. We started with a silent, steady stroke, each one being most careful of his oar, on its entering and leaving the water, and we neither looked to the right nor to the left, nor for a moment turned our heads. After an awful time of suspense in silent steady rowing, we received the signal to slow, and perceiving the boat coming round, as well as hearing the voices of Russians not far away, we felt that we had reached danger point, and for myself I found my heart beating faster. All at once we felt a heavier pull behind us, and we found that our skilful coxswain had come close alongside the boat he had coveted, had noiselessly cut the painter, and we had her in tow. We soon received a signal to put on a faster stroke, when we knew we were on our way back. After a little while we removed the muffles from the oars, for it is not easy work to row long with muffled oars, and we pulled for the shore with all our might. Before we reached our " cove," however, the Russians discovered that something was the matter, for they opened fire in an unusually fierce way. When we had fastened the boats we hurried to our quarters and got to bed. The firing extended along the Russian lines, from the forts to the batteries on the north bank of the river, and it continued throughout the whole night. The allied troops along our front were under arms all night, expecting an attack from the Russians, while perhaps *they* expected the same from the Allies. I slept under a bomb-proof, but in the morning the firing ceased, and we could see how the place had been raked by it.

The coxswain sunk the old boat and blotted out name, number, and everything on the new one which might have betrayed us. It was some days before another flag-of-truce was raised, and the boat wanted. When the officer took his place in the boat he at once found out it was not the old one, and he congratulated the coxswain on providing them with a boat that was safe in which to carry despatches.

Great efforts were made to discover what could have been the cause of that night's firing, but it was never known, nor yet where the boat came from, till the Armistice took place before peace was proclaimed, and then the officer commanding in the town was informed by the coxswain. The officer said it was fortunate for those concerned that it was not found out, as some men had forfeited their lives for less than that.

A GREAT EXPLOSION AND THE DEATH OF A GOOD MAN.

Those who had the principal arrangements for blowing up or otherwise destroying the town, the docks, and the huge warehouses, were anxious to have one grand display of their powers of destruction. To this end, therefore, the concentrated efforts of the sappers and the rest who were working in the town, were directed.

A large square of high buildings and the central docks were selected for this purpose, and the work of mining these at different points was pushed forward. When all was ready for the heavy charges of gunpowder—

great care and privacy were essential in bringing them to the town and in placing them so that the enemy, and others, too, except those actually engaged in the work, should have no knowledge of what was going on. Much of this work, therefore, had to be done in the darkness. When everything was in readiness, the wire connecting the explosive was carried to a place behind the "Malakhoff," which, being attached to a small battery, would give the electric spark to fire the charges.

It was a bright clear morning when the staff came down to the "Malakhoff" to witness this grand, and perhaps final, display of destruction. All who were in the town were warned to leave the place and get to different cover-points by a certain time.

When the signal was given—a small flag raised—the Commander-in-Chief pressed the button which was to start the current, and then there was an awful suspense, for while all were watching to see the effect of the explosion, nothing happened. The engineer officer who had conducted the operations spoke hurriedly to a sergeant who had made the connections with the charges, and the latter assured the officer that everything was right, and that the gunpowder would explode in due time. The officer, however, could not wait, but ran under cover of the wall of the town, until he reached the arched gateway leading into the great square of buildings. As he passed under, the whole block went up, stones being carried to a great dis-

BLOWING UP SEBASTOPOL.

tance all around. It was a grand—awfully grand—sight, but the one absorbing question was, "What had become of the officer?" Some thought he was outside the square and might be alive, but others affirmed that they saw him pass under the gateway, and that he must be buried under the ruins. As soon as possible relays of men began the herculean task of removing the great pile of stones, etc., at the place indicated. For night and day, without any cessation, the work was pushed on, until the remains of the gallant Major Rankin were found.

He was buried in one of the graveyards for English soldiers, with full military honours, and perhaps a stone marks the spot to this day, for I believe these graveyards have been protected, and otherwise attended to, on several occasions since the war.

Many wept as his remains were laid to rest, and especially men of his own regiment, for a braver man never wore soldier's uniform.

AN ARMISTICE.

As the springtime came on, and the days began to lengthen, life in the town of Sebastopol became more bearable. Even the porpoises and other fish came up the harbour, and at times we caught some, and had a refreshing meal.

It was about this time, February, 1856, that the severe strain both to mind and body was relaxed, as a Conference of the contending powers sitting in Paris agreed to an Armistice till the 30th March. It was a great relief to walk about in perfect freedom, after being for months in peril and danger. Boats came from the north side, bringing all kinds of wares and curiosities to barter for money or kind, while all along the banks of the river, inland, men of various nations were fraternizing. Oh, what a contrast between then and a short time before. All hostilities and destructive operations ceased, but there were other kinds of work to be done, such as gathering up the shot to take to our ships for ballast, and in some parts these once deadly missiles lay very thickly on the field. It may not be generally known that the last two men who were killed during this war, and who met their deaths about this time, were an Englishman and a Frenchman. The former was engaged in carrying shot from the field. Artillery men went over the ground first to assort the different kinds, and especially to place unexploded shells by themselves, to be carefully handled by experts. By some mistake, however, one man took up a live shell carrying it on his shoulder until he came to where there was a fire, and then he threw it on the ground in order to light his pipe. No sooner had it struck the ground than it exploded, killing him and injuring several others.

THE PRINCE IMPERIAL.

About this time an event took place, which caused some commotion, not only in the camps of the Allies, but also among the Russians. We were at work one morning in the Redan Fort when a sudden booming of guns was heard in the French lines, which soon extended along the other lines.

It was evident the firing was not connected with combat, but rejoicing, and the men ceased work, declaring that peace was proclaimed. Seeing a cavalryman coming over the hill-crest with all speed towards the town, I ran down to the road, and, as he came near, asked him the news. "Prince of France born," he shouted and sped along. When I told the men, and they had to commence work again, they were very angry, for they had left off and were smoking the pipe of joy.

ANOTHER FREAK.

During the Armistice Russian officers as well as civilians came over to the town, and it was sad to see how some of the former clenched their hands, stamped their feet, or else wept, when they beheld the destruction all around. The most pathetic sight was to see civilians—sometimes women with several children—as they walked among the ruins of some streets. They would stand at different points, and weeping bitterly, would wring their hands, and sometimes tear the hair off their heads. What did it all mean? Perhaps that poor woman with her children, who seemed riveted to the spot in deep anguish, was gazing on what was once their happy home. The awful carnage had probably deprived her of a husband, ruined her homestead, and left her to struggle alone for herself and children. If we multiply this by tens of thousands among the nations who were engaged in the conflict, it would be possible to imagine something of the awful effects of war. My heart ached when I saw such sights, and my sympathy and help were extended to the children, while I longed to get away from such scenes, and hoped never to witness the like again.

I had frequently watched the belching fire from the port-holes of a large fort on the north side, as it had hurled shot and shell over the town, and having been invited to go over and see the place I decided to do so.

I was carefully scanned by the Russians as I landed, and walked towards the fort, for I wore no gay uniform and had no accoutrements. I was the only Englishman who went into the fort at that time, but I was determined to see it, as it was their principal fortification, named "The Star Fort." It was designed and erected by an Englishman, and was considered a splendid piece of work. I was shown over some of the gun chambers, for it would have taken too long to have gone all over the place. Then I was taken into the living-quarters of the soldiers, in the bomb-proof.

I shall never forget my experience, and what I felt while among these men. I no sooner sat down in their midst than I perceived that many of them were ill-disposed towards me. I could only speak a few words of their language, and, therefore, could understand but very little; but I could see by their gestures that some of them were strongly in favour of doing me bodily harm. I thought how foolish I was to enter the place, and wished I was out of it; but it was impossible for me to get out without being shown the way. What was the cause of so many of them appearing to manifest such deadly hatred towards me, and what device could I adopt to get out of the place? These were the two questions that engrossed my mind. In reference to the first question I felt that I had the clue. As I was led into their living-quarters the Russians performed their acts of worship, etc., before the ikon, and several times I was urged to do the same, but did not comply. Then as they handed the strong fiery spirit round I refused to take it. These things may have placed my life in jeopardy, but I afterwards felt that as I had not taken any of the spirit, I was perfectly clearheaded and kept my wits about me. I am thankful that I never took strong drink all the time I was in the Crimea, and I was as healthy and strong as most men.

Now, what stratagem could I adopt to get out of the place, for I could see that some of them were getting maddened with drink? There was one who appeared superior to the rest, and I think he came in after I entered, and I did not see him drink. So I represented to him how delighted I was with all I had seen, and offered to give the men presents—small coins, etc.— and beckoned him to show me the way out, and while those who were intoxicated were making a terrible noise, and quarrelling, he led me out! I was glad to get safely back to my own quarters, and while I did not think much about my escape at the time, I have often since then recognized the protecting hand of God.

PEACE REJOICINGS.

As the month's Armistice drew towards a close much anxiety was felt as to whether it would bring peace, or whether hostilities would be resumed. On the appointed day the glad tidings of peace were proclaimed throughout the whole lines, by the booming of guns and universal rejoicing.

A general fraternizing now began among both officers and men of the once opposing nations. It was arranged that a great farewell gathering should take place on a certain day, on the plains of the Tchernaya. It was a wonderful sight to see the thousands gathered together in friendly intercourse, and engaged in all kinds of sports—including horse-racing—the staff officers of the various nations competing. I never witnessed such a sight before, nor have I seen such a gathering since. There were men there belonging to over twenty different nationalities, and I suppose every one was heartily glad that the war was over.

The Allies now began to evacuate the place as fast as vessels could take them away.

On our arrival in England I had to appear at the War Office to settle accounts, and get my discharge.

I received a nice sum of money to balance my pay sheet, and should have had much more only there was a large deduction as my share of payment for the schooner that conveyed us from Tunis to Malta— before referred to.

It was with mingled feelings of joy and sadness that I visited the place of my birth. As soon as possible I called at the Vicarage to see my best friend and his wife and daughter. They accorded me a very warm welcome. As they sat and looked, first at me, and then at each other, I saw they were nearly moved to tears, for I suppose they were thinking of the time when I left them, a poor friendless orphan lad.

IMPORTANT EVENTS.

Two important events happened during this decade. One of these was the very happy union between myself and the young woman whom God graciously gave me for my wife. For more than a quarter of a century she was my faithful companion, the sharer of my joys and sorrows; an unwearied co-worker in my missionary labours, a devoted wife, and a most affectionate mother —for she brought up six children. The other event was my conversion to God, a passing from death unto Life, being '' Born again of the Spirit.''

For several years I was engaged in different situations in London, and at length I found employment in a large '' Marine Engineers' Firm,'' where there were, when business was good, from 600 to 800 men, and here it was that—what I may call, and which in reality it was—the greatest event of my life took place.

SPIRITUAL AWAKENING.

I always had the fear of God before me, and felt a restraining power that kept me back from rushing into open and flagrant sins, but I had never had my eyes opened to see myself as a guilty, hell-deserving sinner. My conversion came about in this way.

A London City Missionary went to visit a row of houses near the factory in which I worked, and in one of these lived a notorious man, named Ned Weeks. The missionary had sought many opportunities to get a talk with the man, but the latter would never see him. Ned could not read, but as his wife could the missionary would select a suitable tract, and ask her to read it to her husband, praying God would bless it to the man. Ned worked in the same part of the factory as myself. He was by far the most terrible man in the works, and was a desperate fighter. He was wholly abandoned, and gave himself up, without restraint, to every sin and vice. Ned had been cradled, reared, trained, and daily practised in evil ever since he could remember, till it had become an important part of his daily life, aye, and his living, too. He never had a day's schooling, for as soon as Ned could walk, his father took him in charge, and as he was the first-born he was going to train him up to be "a man" who could take his own part and find his way in the world.

They lived at Dartford, in Kent, and the father had an extensive knowledge of horses, understood their points well, could manage them, and doctor them if they were ailing. He was a most powerful man, a heavy drinker, and a pugilist. For many years he drove the " Bank-note " van to London, three times a week, up to town one day, and back again the next.

As soon as Ned was old enough he went in the van with his father and became habituated to drinking and fighting. He not only had to witness his father fight, but often to fight lads himself, his father teaching him how to defeat them.

Now that Ned was a father himself, with a wife and three little children, he fully practised all that his father had taught him. He appeared to care nothing for his home and family. When he was not at work he was in the " tap-room." The only things that he wanted home for was to have his food and take his sleep in. Sunday was generally a busy day, for he said he could often earn more money on that day than he earned all the week at the works. The whole day was spent in visiting stables, advising about, or giving medicine to horses, for, like his father, he was very clever in these things. His family was none the better for all his takings, and his children were in an awfully deplorable condition, all owing to drink.

He was like his father, a powerful man, and could get through his hard work as well as anyone. He was hot-tempered, and nearly every day found him in some brawl or other; therefore it was no uncommon thing for him to be engaged in fights, in the dinner hour, or at night outside the factory gates, and I never knew him to be defeated.

Such was the kind of man that Mr. S——, the City missionary, was seeking to bring into a new and better life. He knew a great deal of Ned's abandoned and vicious life, for no one could enter his so-called home and see the wretched condition of his family but would have the fact powerfully borne in upon him that the man who could permit things to drift to such a state, and had the power to alter it, and would not, must indeed be almost beyond hope. The missionary's hope, however, was in God, and so he kept on striving and praying, believing, hoping, watching, and at length he saw a little sign which impelled him to continue his laudable efforts.

Ned had frequently told his wife what he would do to the missionary if he caught him in the house, but the tracts were still left, and Ned felt the tremendous home-thrusts in his conscience. "What does the missionary want with me?" he asked one day. His wife replied, "He says he would like you to be a better and a happier man." "Well, anyhow, he sticks well to his job, and as nothing seems to shake him off, I'll see him if he calls when I'm in," said Ned. From that time they came to what may be termed "close quarters." The conflict was long, for the great enemy, Satan, would not easily lose such a life-long doughty soldier from his ranks. One Sunday night he attended a service conducted by an evangelist—the late Wm. Carter—and there he made a full surrender to Christ.

This man was the instrument whom God, in His Sovereign grace and mercy, used in bringing me to a saving knowledge of Himself. The morning after his conversion, as soon as he came to his work, I could see that Ned was a different man, and when I spoke to him he said, "I've done with the old service, now I belong to Jesus Christ, and whether I live or die it does not matter, I am His, and He is mine."

These words completely stunned me, and for a time I stood speechless. The thoughts that passed through my mind—much faster than I can write them—were these : Here is a man who has never had parents or Christian teachers to train him in good things when a boy, who has never been to Sunday School, who cannot read the Bible, who has lived in utter ignorance of God, His Word, and His Holy religion, and here am I, with all the advantages that I have had, and yet if he die to-day he is safe for heaven, and if I die I shall be lost for ever. Ned told me what he had been through the previous night, "but," he added, "you can read the Book, and that will show you what to do." I was very anxious to get home that day, so that I could read my Bible, the same one that was given me when I left the Sunday School, and which I have in my bed-room now, while I am writing these lines, it being the only thing that has gone through life with me.

THE DARKNESS DEEPENS.

Arriving home that day, instead of greeting my wife, and entering the house with a cheery smile, and bounding step, I was sad and dejected. My dear wife was somewhat alarmed as I could eat no food, and looked so awfully wretched. I found my Bible, and shut myself in the bed-room, and falling on my knees tried to pray, but I could only agonize and weep. I opened the Book, and began to read, but every sentence seemed to plunge the sword of Divine Justice deeper into my poor wounded spirit. The night was passed in bitter anguish of soul, and when the light of day came it brought no relief. Ned tried his best to help me in the meal times by telling me of his new found joy, his very countenance beaming with the light and peace that filled his soul. But this only deepened the awful darkness of my spirit. The evil one suggested that the Book might be wrong, and after all I might be right, for I had not been such a vile sinner as some had been, not even as my friend Ned, and, therefore, why trouble about it, for I should certainly be right in the end. I was convinced, however, that the Book was right, and that I was wrong. Yes, I could see clearly my own condemnation, and the sentence of death was passed at the bar of my conscience; and many times, during those days of darkness and distress, did I really wish that God would take away my life, and shut me up in hell. Taking very little food, and being scarcely able to perform my duties by day, and getting hardly any rest at night, in bitter anguish of spirit as to the past, and dark despair as to the future—yet withal keeping to the Book and crying to God—the days and nights of the week passed. Now if my readers will try to conceive what such a week as I passed through must be to body, mind, and spirit, they will understand somewhat my meaning when I say that on Saturday I was completely exhausted. My dear wife became seriously alarmed when she saw my utter collapse, and begged me to try and get relief. I told her to get my Sunday clothes ready for the morning, for I felt I must go somewhere or die. The next day I arose early, and wandered up and down the long main road. At length I saw a number of people going into a House of Prayer, and I passed in among them.

THE DAWN OF DAY.

This Sabbath was destined to be a memorable one to my soul, for, during the day, I was brought out of darkness into God's marvellous Light. No sooner was the hymn sung, and prayer offered, than a ray of light, of hope, entered my soul. The sermon was evidently prepared for cases such as mine, and the preacher directed his attention, and urged his plea, entirely on me—so I thought—and I drank in every word. The subject was "looking to Christ." He expounded what Faith was, and how, by resting on

Christ, and His Atoning Sacrifice, salvation could be attained by any poor sinner.

When I reached home I got my Bible, and as I read it increasing light shone from its sacred pages, and the black clouds of despair began to roll away. In the afternoon my friend Ned and others called on me, and I went to a little Mission service. In the evening I was early to the House of God, for, oh, how I panted for deliverance. The prayers and praises of the congregation were to my soul like the refreshing rain on the parched ground, while the sermon based on the parable of " The barren fig tree," was applied to my heart by the power and grace of the Holy Spirit. In the after-meeting I was pointed to Christ, as my atoning Lord and Saviour, and by simply trusting— wholly trusting—Him, my heart o'erflowed with peace, and joy, and love. In a word, I entered into a full, free, and present salvation.

All things then became new to me—new heavens and a new earth, and new views of God. His love flooded my whole being, and I could not help but talk, and sing, of such amazing love to me a poor sinner, in such strains as these :—

" Oh, 'twas love, 'twas wondrous love,
    The love of God to me ;
It brought my Saviour from above,
    To die on Calvary."

I also had new views of the Holy Scriptures. I had read them in my childhood, but now the Book was pregnant with Life and blessings; the previous week every page seemed black with condemnation (to me), but now those same pages glowed with light, and hope, and love.

Yes, Christ, and His redemptive work, seemed to stand out in bold relief on every page, for judgments, precepts, and promises were sign-posts pointing to Christ. At this time the Bible had such a power over me that it completely "gripped" me. I really felt it was waste of time to read anything else. I literally hungered and thirsted for the Word of the Living God, and every opportunity I had its sacred pages were opened. Three times a day I read some portion on my knees, praying God to enlighten my mind and give me understanding in eternal verities.

My change of heart and life soon became known to some Christian people, among whom were ministers, and I was inundated with piles of books to read on doctrine, theology, creeds, etc., but at this time I had no desire for these things. For twelve months—and I note this with a thankful heart for myself, and trust it may be a help to some who may see these lines, in this rushing, reading age—I read no other book but the Bible. I read the New Testament and parts of the Old very carefully, and with earnest prayer for light and wisdom. The Epistle to the Romans appeared so important for understanding the Religion of Jesus Christ, that I was drawn towards it as by magnetic power, and read it through three times with prayerful meditation, until I could clearly see the way of Salvation through Jesus Christ, of how God " might be just, and the justifier of him which believeth in Jesus."

How thankful I have been all along the subsequent years, that I was guided for the first twelve months in that way, for no sophistry, or subtle infidel argument, could move me from the one true foundation, and by the grace of God I have been enabled to use that Word with some effect in my Mission work.

WITNESS-BEARING IN THE WORKSHOP.

I can never forget the first morning I entered the factory after my conversion. Ned and I had a little prayer together before the bell rang for the day's work to begin. I believed that everyone to whom I had the opportunity of speaking would at once accept the salvation of Christ, but the day had not far advanced before I had to meet with ridicule, derision, and mocking, and as the news spread of the change in both of us, the forces of evil gathered about us. The leaders of infidelity and of various vices hurled their curses and blasphemies at us in a most relentless manner. Their onslaughts were so rapid and full of derision and scorn that we could only keep quiet, and in patience possess our souls. It soon became evident that a united phalanx of opponents was banded together to knock this out of us, or make it too hot for us to remain there. Arguments used on Ned were answered by his own experience—for he could not read—and one illus-

IN A FACTORY.

tration will suffice to show how it was done. At dinner time a number of men—and among them two of the foreman's sons—commenced on my friend, and with taunts and jeers, with curses and blasphemies, denounced Christ, the Bible, religion, and himself as a base hypocrite. I trembled for my brother, as I could see the conflict raging within, and I knew that if he were to commence to deal with them as a short time ago he would have done, our cause would suffer. I besought him to keep calm and kept praying, and I soon saw he had got the victory over himself, for his face beamed with pity towards them, and stepping close up to them he held up his hand and spoke somewhat as follows :—

" May I say a word? " " Yes," they replied.

" Most of you men have known me for some time, and I suppose you believe I'm Ned Weeks. Now can you tell me what has happened, for me to stand here and listen to all the names you have called me, and for not one of you to have been knocked down? " No answer came. Then he told them what had caused the change, and that he only wished they all knew the same blessed experience. . All went to their work to think, and one said, " That which has produced such a change like this in Ned, must be good."

In my own case their onslaughts were somewhat different, though quite as bitter. Arguments from infidel writers, and debates against Christianity, were brought forward, and especially as they declared the supposed contradictions, false statements, and impossibilities found in the Bible. Among the many questions asked—some of which I did not attempt to answer, they being too profane or blasphemous—was one by a very intelligent and well-educated man, and it was whether I really believed that God could forgive a man's sin, however bad he had been? I answered "Yes." "Now," said he, "you believe the Bible to be true, do you not?" "Quite true," I answered. "The Bible says that the soul that sinneth shall die." "Yes," I replied. "Then," said he, "if God forgives a sinner when He has declared the soul that sinneth must die, how can He be just?" In a most remarkable manner my tongue was unloosed to proclaim the love of God, in giving Jesus to come into the world to die for sinners, and that on the ground of His substitutionary work, God could be just and the Justifier of all who truly repented of their sins, and trusted in Christ. All they said in reply was, they did not believe it, and yet I am thankful to say that the man who asked the question afterwards became truly converted to God.

For months the opposition and sometimes bitter persecution continued, but we kept to the Bible, and as I have said, I devoted all the time I had to studying its sacred pages. I got a copy of the New Testament to read to my friend Ned in the early morning, and at meal-times, the truths of which he drank in with a thirst, the like of which I have never witnessed. A most remarkable thing in my case was—and I thankfully record it for the encouragement of those who have the training and teaching of children—that no sooner was I converted from the error of my ways than the knowledge of the Holy Scriptures, and the religion of Jesus Christ which I had acquired when a boy, all seemed to come back to me.

Our friend, the London City Missionary, of course, took a lively interest in us both, and we used to attend his Bible Class, and other meetings, and notwithstanding our many slips and stumbles—for the enemy got the advantage of one or the other of us at different times—he was a faithful and skilful shepherd in applying the healing balm of God's Word, when either of us was injured by the adversary. He also invited us to go to the open-air meetings. These were stirring times, and I was frequently put forward to give out a hymn and sometimes to speak. Ned was also asked to give his experience, and, when he did so, numbers would stop and listen to his thrilling story, and gaze on his radiant face, for it shone with a heavenly lustre while he was speaking. Mr. S——, the Missionary, received an appointment to go out to West Africa in connection with a Foreign Missionary Society. His last words to me, as he held my hand and said, "Goodbye," were, "Now make haste and get into the work, and give heed to God's call." He was at his station in Africa only six months when he fell a victim to the deadly fever, and his beloved partner and helpmeet returned home a lonely widow. She lived to a great age, and it was my joy to call upon her occasionally and render what little comfort and succour I was able.

A few weeks after my conversion my dear wife was brought to a saving knowledge of the truth, and for awhile our pathway to the skies seemed to be strewn with flowers. Our Gracious and loving Father, however, saw fit to place us in the fires, and also to bring us through deep waters, and while, at the time it was most trying both to body and soul, I have thanked God many times since then for the way He brought me.

AFFLICTION.

Some time after this I was taken ill with fever, and could not work for months, and, strange to say, the side where I had the tumour when a boy was now swollen to a great size. The doctor said I must go to the hospital and undergo an operation, but my dear wife would not consent. I got worse, and the doctor said there was no hope of my getting well again, and Christian friends came to see me, believing it would be the last time. My good friend Ned came almost every night, to try and comfort my wife, and pray with me, and on one of these occasions he seemed so full of rapture at the thought of my being so near heaven, that in his prayer he thanked God that I should be safe landed in glory before morning, and began to sing, "There'll be no more sorrow there." This was more than my poor wife could bear, and she told Ned not to come and pray like that again, for she felt he was in a greater hurry to get me into heaven than God was. "I believe," she exclaimed, "that God will spare my husband to do a noble work for Him yet, for I pray continually for him, and feel convinced that God, in His mercy, will raise him up for me and these little children to serve Him."

It was made known to the men in the factory that the doctor had said that I could not recover, and so, unknown to myself, or anyone connected with me, several of them agreed to come and see me. One evening three of them came, the sceptical son of the foreman, who was the one who always led the attacks on religion, and two others from the same department.

They stood around my bed, and with a smile I was just able to say how glad I was to see them. For a few moments they said nothing, but looked at each other; at length the leader said, "We understand you can never rise from this bed again, and we would like to know if you have the hope and assurance now which you told us you had when at work?" My little Testament was under my pillow, and I took it in my hand, and looking at them I said, "George, this is God's Word, and every promise is true. I have given up all to Christ, if I live, I live to Him, if I die, I go to Him, whether living or dying I am His. Tell the men at the factory that I have no fear, but am perfectly happy." For a time they appeared to be rivetted to the spot and were speechless, then looking at my wife and the babe in her arms, the tears stood in their eyes while George said, '' We believe what you say, and hope you will get better for the sake of your little family,'' and they bade me farewell.

I cannot tell what the immediate effect of the visit was upon the three men, but I am thankful to record that two of them afterwards became followers of the Saviour.

SEVERE TESTS OF FAITH.

As my affliction continued, so the floods seemed to surge around us, and deepen, till it appeared as though we should be overwhelmed. The Apostle Peter says, '' That the trial of your faith, being much more precious than gold that perisheth, though it be tried with fire, might be found unto praise, and honour, and glory, at the appearing of Jesus Christ.''

Yes, it was a severe trial to the faith of both myself and my dear wife, for as soon as I was taken ill my wages stopped, and we were soon at the end of our resources. We had three little children, and our cupboards were often empty, and my beloved partner struggled hard for a bit of bread, and would not let me know the worst in my pain and weakness. The way, however, that God interposed to supply our need was marvellous, and I record but a little of it, to His praise and glory. I have often thought that it is easy to sing '' Faith, mighty faith, the promise sees, and looks to that alone,'' when the larder is well replenished, but it is not so easy to do so when hungry little children are crying round their mother for bread, and she knows not which way to turn to obtain it.

My wife was skilful at needle work, but with a sick husband and three small children, if she worked night and day—that is, all the time she could crowd in—she could do but little. As our case became desperate we could only cast ourselves more fully on God in prayer, and the way that God helped us was on the margin of the miraculous, if not quite so.

One day our little boys were crying with hunger, and their mother told them to run down the street while she finished some work, and then she would get them some bread. They had not been out many minutes before a woman, who was a near neighbour, came to the door and said to my wife, " Mrs. Dunn, you ought to give your little boy a good thrashing, for he has taken my child's bread and butter out of his hand and eaten it all."

My dear wife burst into tears, and said, " I can't beat him, Mrs. M——, for he has not had a bit of food since yesterday."

The woman then came in, and after enquiring all about our state, said, " My husband is a baker, and we always have a loaf a day more than we want, and we will gladly give it you." She at once went and brought some food, and the children had a meal, and God was thanked.

ALL AVENUES CLOSED.

On some occasions the outlook was extremely dark for my brave partner, and, to add to her distress, the doctor kept urging her to let me be taken to the hospital for an operation, or I should certainly die. One Saturday evening the doctor called, and as I had been delirious for a long time, he strongly urged his plea, but my dear wife said, '' No, doctor, he shall not go, and if he dies he shall die at home.'' After awhile I rallied from a composing sleep, was again conscious, and certainly seemed a little better. My wife sat at the bedside crying, and when I asked the reason for it, she said :—

'' This is Saturday night, and I've washed the children and put them to bed, but I was wondering what we shall do, for we have no food, and to-morrow is Sunday.''

I told her to get the Bible and read a little, which she did, and then we prayed. I then said :—

'' We can only trust, and wait, and our Father knows I am here and cannot help myself, and so we must just look to Him.''

The clock struck eleven, and my dear wife said, '' What shall we do? The children will wake in the morning hungry, and I have no food, and the shops will soon close. What *can* we do?''

At this juncture, and the midnight hour approaching, a knock came at the door, and on my wife opening it a youth with a large basket of provisions asked if Mrs. Dunn lived there? "Yes," she answered, "I'm that person." "I was told," he said, "to bring these things to you; let me have the basket quickly, as they will be shutting up soon." He did not know who ordered the things, and we could not find out, nor do I know to this day. I need not say that our hearts were filled with gratitude, and my dear wife wept for very joy as she looked at her store—for we had everything that was necessary for our present requirements. As the midnight hour struck we were thanking and praising God, and resolving that we would never distrust our gracious Father again.

The Sabbath dawned, and the children laughed when they saw their mother putting the food on the table for their breakfast, and looked amazed when she told them, in answer to their questions, that God had sent it. We had a very happy day, and we could not have been happier had we possessed a purse full of money and a well-stocked larder, for had not our loving Father come to our aid just when we needed?

We had not a doubt but that He would do so in every time of need in the future. Our friend Ned, with several others, called to see me, and when he heard of God's interposition in our behalf, he simply said, "I knew God would help you in some way, for while I was praying on Saturday night I felt so happy." Prayer and praise ascended to God from my sick chamber, and all felt that God was present.

DIVINE INTERPOSITIONS.

It would fill a volume to relate all the gracious providential interpositions in our behalf during my long and painful illness, but one other wonderful instance I must relate. The most pressing difficulty with my devoted wife was the rent, for while we could go short of many things, the landlord's claim must be met. He was paid a little at a time, as my hard toiling partner could earn the money. But, with all her efforts, the debt for rent kept increasing, and it looked—from a human standpoint—as though our little home would be taken away. On the eve of the day, when it was feared this might happen, a well-to-do tradesman, whom we had known since our conversion, called at our house late, and said,

"Mrs. Dunn, I don't know how you are circumstanced, but I passed by the end of your street three times, and was each time impelled to turn back, for something seemed to say, 'Go and see how that poor man is.' I thought on two of these occasions, why, it's too late to-night, I will call another time, but on the third time I came along. Now, tell me, is your husband worse, or what is the matter?"

My poor wife at first could not speak for weeping, but at length she told him I was no worse.

"Ah, well," he said, "I'm sure there is something," and thrusting his hand into his pocket he emptied its contents on the table, saying, "that may be of some little help to you; tell your husband I will call and see him another day," and he opened the door and left.

My dear wife gathered up the money and came up to the sick-room exclaiming,

" See what the Lord has sent us, more than will pay the landlord."

She then told me how our good friend and benefactor —for he became a real benefactor to us after this—was constrained by the Spirit to come to our help in this our pressing need. Again we united in praising God for this timely aid. When the landlord came the rent was fully paid, and we went forward rejoicing.

No one can have any adequate conception of the great strain, both mental and physical, as well as the severe trial to one's faith, of passing through a series of such straitened times, unless some similar circumstances have been experienced. Still, it is worth all the strain, the hardships, and the agony, to have the unspeakable joy of such gracious and Divine interpositions with all their strengthening and upraising power.

Will the reader consider that for more than four months we were passing through these waters of affliction, and that in every time of stress and need we experienced the Divine interposition.

The greatest benefit to myself—as seen from my present standpoint—was the experience I had then, in fitting me for service in this Mission, where tenderness of heart for those in distress, sympathy with those in affliction and sorrow, a prayerful watching for, and a willing outstretched hand to help those in special need, are pre-eminently necessary to comfort the many weary and sad hearts the missionary has to meet.   Many times have I thanked God for past experience.

FURTHER CONFLICTS.

It was a happy morning for my old friend Ned when he saw me enter the factory and commence work after my long and trying illness. He had had to battle alone with the phalanx of opponents, and, although unable to read, he had mighty faith in God and His salvation, which proved more than a match for his assailants. One of their stock arguments was, if God was such a loving Father as he had said, how was it that I had had such a painful affliction, and my family brought to want? My good friend could only say that he could not understand it, but he believed it was all right, if not, God would have ordered it otherwise. They could not but admit that his faith was marvellous, and his life to them was most remarkable.

As time went on, and our zeal in work for Christ was intensified, both inside the works and also outside, in the open-air and in Mission Rooms—one of which was close to the factory, and before long was too small to admit the numbers gathered there—so the enemy became more determined to hinder, or, if possible, to stop God's work altogether

One of the managers said to me one day,

" I hear that you have turned ' psalm singer,' and go ranting about this place, and also outside. Now, if you don't give up this canting hypocritical stuff, you will have to leave this place, and carry it on somewhere else, so you must make your choice." Looking at him, I said,

" Yes, sir, it is quite true that my course of life has been changed, and my conduct is not the same as formerly, but you don't dismiss men, sir, because they change their opinions, for there are a great variety of opinions here. If, however, you find anything in my duties to justify your dismissing me, I will go."

" I shall soon find that," he said, and left me.

It did not take long for my friend and me to find out that we were the objects of scrutiny, not only by the men we were working with, but also by those in authority, and so we asked God daily to help us to be true and faithful witness-bearers for Him in life and conduct, as well as by our conversation. Various accusations were brought against one or both of us from time to time. Sometimes it would be reported that our work was scamped, but, thank God, that always proved false, because we had resolved that what was done should bear the fullest scrutiny, both as to quantity and quality.

It was also rumoured that we were the meanest and most niggardly men in the works. This was because we did not squander our money away in drink and gambling. This latter charge was overthrown once

for all, on our pay-day.   One of our men, a poor fellow
with a wife and family, had met with a serious accident, and was taken to the hospital.   The son of the
foreman in our department decided to have a collection among the men for his family.   Tom was always
a favourite with those who attended tap-rooms
and concert halls, and joined heartily with those
who ridiculed our religion.   Ned had already
visited the wife and children, and, unknown to
our workmates, had helped them.   The appeal
was written at the head of the paper, and the
list of subscriptions was started by the chief mechanics,
some of whom earned from four to six pounds weekly.
The collecting was placed in the hands of two men
who could bounce or bully men into giving more, if
they thought they had not given enough.   It took some
time to go round with the list, as before the men gave
to this object, money which had been borrowed had to
be repaid, the drink-bill settled, and money lost in bet-
ting and gambling squared.   We waited quietly, as we
had heard they would not ask us, and at the end of
the round they came and said, "Could we give a
trifle to Tom's wife and family?"   "Certainly," I
replied, and wrote my name for so much; then Ned
said, "Put me down for the same amount."   The
collectors looked at one another and said, "We ought
to have started here, and then we should have collected
more money."   Afterwards, if a man met with an accident, and a collection was to be made, Ned and myself

were asked to make it, as they said we could get the largest collection for the man.

By patient endurance, by strict attention and fidelity to duty, and by seeking to manifest the Christ-like spirit to all men, much of the opposition was overcome in course of time. Many of the men began to think and enquire about this new life, and some of them became converted to God, while a few of the " dormant " Christians in the firm seemed to wake up, and rejoice at what their eyes saw, and their ears heard, of the wonderful workings of the Holy Spirit in the factory. My friend Ned was recommended to fill an important position of trust in the firm, while in the department where I worked, if anything of a special nature, or work requiring care and attention had to be done, I was mostly entrusted with the duty of seeing it carried out. So marvellously did God vindicate His own cause, and that of His servants in this place. One of our friends who was converted here was selected— out of some hundreds—to fill an important post at Manilla, in the Philippines, and rose to a high position under the Spanish Government. But while the opposition to our faith and conduct was broken down, the testing time was always with us.

THE SABBATH FOR MAN.

The Sabbath was to me a day of great joy and delight, for I was trying to work for our Divine Lord from early morn till late at night. I began to take appointments to preach in different places, and, as time went on, these increased. In the busy season, when engines had to be completed by a certain time, or in cases of some break-down in a mail boat, overtime had to be continued through the night. Work had to be done occasionally on Sundays; the men usually did not mind this, as they were paid for double time.

At one such time, when we were being paid at 4 o'clock on Saturday, we were asked to come back after tea to work. It was on this occasion that I had a rather severe trial of faith. It was about 10 o'clock when we were informed that we must work all night and the next day, Sunday. Some of them said,

"Now you will see where his religion will go; for if he does not stay and work he will be dismissed, and if he does, we shall not believe any more in *his* religion."

I heard these things, but said nothing; the conflict, however, was going on within. A short time before midnight I went out into the darkness of the night and lifted up my heart to God for help and guidance, and I at once felt what course I ought to take—under all the circumstances, and resolved to take it. As I returned to work all eyes were turned towards me, but a little before midnight, I went to the Manager and said,

"As you are aware, sir, some time ago I began to serve God, and as He has set apart one day out of the seven to worship and serve Him—the Sabbath—I must ask permission to leave work now."

With a stern voice he replied, " Well, if that is your determination and you go, I won't promise you another day's work."

" I *must* go, sir," I replied, " and the issue I can leave with God," and so I bade them good-night.

The next day—Sunday—I had a full and happy day's service for God. I went to my work as usual on Monday morning, while some of those who worked on Sunday did not come in at all, but were drinking, and several kept it up for a few days longer. I heard nothing further about the affair from the manager until a few weeks after, when one Saturday he said to me, " Will you come back to work to-night, James? You can leave off, you know, at your own time." Thus it happened that I was never again asked to work on Sundays.

God's work among the men spread marvellously, and some were won for Christ in a remarkable way. Many instances might be given, but I will only refer to one. Several of us were engaged one day in work that was very dangerous, having to pass to and from a certain place with great care. One man in the gang was very bitter against religion, and was " exceeding mad " against those who professed it. I did not know until afterwards that this man had laid a trap to injure me, or it might be, to cause my death. Now, it so happened that in coming by this place he himself fell and was severely hurt, and being in danger of his life, cried out for help. His boon companions did not care to jeopardize themselves, so asked me if I could extricate him. I succeeded in getting the poor fellow out at no little risk to myself, and when I laid him down in the air, he had fainted. A conveyance was brought and he was taken home.

On the following Sunday afternoon I went to see him, and I shall never forget the scene when I entered his bed-room. As soon as he saw me he burst out crying, and stretching out his hands, exclaimed,

"Oh, James, will you forgive me? I have had no peace since they brought me home, will you forgive me?"

I told him I had nothing to forgive, but he must ask God to forgive his past sins.

"I have been doing that all the time I have been here, but you know how I tried to injure you, don't you? That trap I laid for you, I fell into myself, and but for you I might have been in eternity now, and lost. Will you forgive me?"

I sat down by his bed-side, and taking his hands in mine, said,

"Dry up those tears, George, I have nothing to forgive you for; God takes care of me from day to day, for 'whether I live, I live to Him, and whether I die, I die to Him; whether living or dying I am the Lord's.' Now I want you to trust wholly in Christ, and you shall be in His safe keeping in life and in death."

I read the Scriptures and directed him to the "Lamb of God Which taketh away the sin of the world." His contrition was deep, and he wept most of the time I was reading and speaking, and it was only after we had prayed together that light broke in, and he entered into peace, and rest, through believing. He recovered and went back to his employment, but we did not work together again, and some time after he left the neighbourhood, and appeared to be living a truly consistent life.

MORE IMPORTANT EVENTS.

Several events happened about this time which had momentous issues, to one or two of which I will refer. I was often requested to take Sunday services at Mission Halls and Chapels, and to speak at gatherings of working people on week days. Mr. H. Whybrow—a Christian man—had arranged for a meeting of his workpeople in his warehouse in Well Close Square, and I was asked to speak. He had invited several of his friends to the gathering, and among them was that very successful Missionary to Thieves, in connection with the London City Mission, Mr. Thomas Jackson.

My soul was all on fire, and I was enabled to tell out of an overflowing heart what God had done for me, and to urge the claims of Christ on all present. Many were broken down, and the presence of Christ was there to heal; not that such a thing was uncommon, for a mighty revival wave was passing over London at this time.

On another occasion I was asked to give an address

to a company of thieves gathered for a service in a large room in Mr. Jackson's house. After the service it was customary for Mr. Jackson to invite any who were desirous of giving up their evil course of life to remain behind for prayer, and some very remarkable cases were dealt with. I could give some remarkable instances in point, but I must forbear.

A CALL TO MISSION WORK.

Shortly after the events recorded in the preceding pages I received from the Secretary of the London City Mission the usual forms to Candidates, with a letter asking me to fill in the answers, and forward them to the Mission House, 3, Red Lion Square. Several Missionaries, including Mr. Jackson, saw me on the subject, and urged me to consider whether this was not a call from God. After much prayer and consultation with Christian ministers and friends, I filled in the papers and sent them on to the Secretary. I heard nothing further for some months, as my papers had been overlooked, and in the meantime I went on with my work, thinking no more about the matter. All my spare time on Sundays and week-days was fully occupied in work for God, and I was very happy. One morning, however, I received a letter from the Secretary—the Rev. John Robinson—apologizing for having overlooked my papers, and asking me to call and see him.

This closes the third decade of my life, truly a most eventful one, and from this point I start upon what may be called my real life-work.

> " Here I raise my Ebenezer,
>   Hither by Thy help, I've come."

FOURTH DECADE.

In all my former experiences I never felt such heart-stirrings as I did when entering upon the work of the London City Mission. Yet I felt that God, Who had guided and helped me hitherto, would continue to do so until the end, and having put my hand to the plough I dared not look back. I was sent to four Clerical Examiners, Dr. Angus, Dr. Edmunds, Dr. Lorimer, and the Rev. Aubrey Price, and having satisfied them I was told to give the required notice to the firm where I was employed, in order to be ready to start mission work.

The last few weeks in the factory were full of stirring incidents. Old antagonists were earnestly pleaded with to turn to God before it was too late. I found out afterwards that some became Christians, but others also continued their mocking. One of these latter, an unmarried man, who could earn in busy seasons from four to five pounds weekly, said to me :—

" James, I don't think much of your Father that you are always talking about. He does not seem to care much about you, to let you do such work as that. I would sooner be a slave in South America than do what you have to do."

" Well, John," I replied, " I've often heard you say,

' what's the odds, so long as you are happy.' Now, do you think I am happy?''

" Oh, yes," said he, " we all know you are happy enough."

" Well, now," I rejoined, " if it pleases God to keep me at this work until my hair is white, I can do it to His glory, and feel happy; but if He sees fit to take me from it, and put me somewhere else, He can do so. Can you say, John, that you are happy in your present state?'' (I knew he had just returned from a few weeks " on the spree," as he called it, and had lost over twenty pounds.)

" No," he said emphatically, " I'm not, I wish I was."

I told him once again how he could obtain the blessing.

" You are right," he exclaimed. " I must think about it, for it's a long lane that has no turning."

I urged him to turn before he got to the end, but in about a fortnight after I left he was carried off with cholera.

Before my term expired, the principal partner in the firm sent for me to the counting-house. Asking my name, he told me that the minister of the Church he attended—the Rev. Aubrey Price—had told him that I was about to become a London City Missionary. He thought he would like to see me in order to say how pleased he was that I was going to start in such a good cause. He asked many questions, and I told him of some of the men who were living witnesses for Christ in the works. This gave him much joy.

When my notice had expired I went to the Mission House, and after some instructions from the Secretary, I was appointed to a district in Bethnal Green.

MARCHING ORDERS.

The Rev. John Robinson—one of the Secretaries—placed a Bible in my hands, and told me that that must be the weapon to use in my work, both for offensive and defensive purposes. He said that the district to which I was appointed—Virginia Row, Bethnal Green—was one of the worst in London, and that my work was to seek to make known the Gospel to every person in the district, by visiting the homes and workshops in every street, court, and alley, from garret to cellar, adding, "Mind you go to the top of the house first, and then you will be sure to find your way to the bottom—even if you should be thrown down."

A thorough inspection of my appointed corner in the great harvest-field of London was the first thing I attempted in my new sphere.

The district was four square, comprising several streets, some courts and blind alleys, a chapel with a burying ground behind it, both closed; and a dust yard into which was brought the refuse from the parish, where sorting, sifting, and burning of all kinds of abominable stuff was carried on daily, mostly by women. On the north side of the district was a large area of slums, which was quite a maze, from which, if a stranger advanced far, he would find it extremely difficult to get out again. A wide road was cut from east to west, through what was called the "Burker's ground," so named on account of a species of murder which left no mark of violence on the bodies of the victims, which were afterwards sold to surgeons for dissection. The first known criminal by whom it was perpetrated was a man named Burke. A large square of this dangerous area was afterwards cleared away, and artisans' dwellings erected, with a church, and ultimately a fish market. The first and last of these were called respectively, Columbia Square and Columbia Market. These improvements were carried out by Miss, afterwards the Baroness, Burdett-Coutts. The Market was opened by the proprietress in 1869, at a cost of over £200,000, but it was never a success, and in 1871 the Baroness presented it to the Corporation of London.

I started in real earnest on my new work, beginning at one corner and visiting every house in every street and court, and, as far as possible, every family in every house. Daily contact with open sin and vice, constant threatenings with oaths and blasphemies, mocking and jeering on every hand, hardness of heart and contempt of the Word of God, were most trying to one's faith, and often I returned home at night depressed in spirit and body, to weep and pray over the sin and indifference of the -people. But I was much sustained and encouraged to persevere in my work by the sympathy and prayers of my devoted wife, who became a real help to me in my arduous task.

SUSPECTED.

In course of time I was able to gain the confidence of some of the people, while here and there were to be found a few of the Lord's "hidden ones," but the greater number seemed to suspect me a little as a "spy" coming to have their courts and alleys swept away, or else as a government detective, to entrap unwary criminals. These ideas were so deeply rooted in the minds of many that it took several years before I was accepted as a true man.

No doubt the reason of all this was that so many were leading unlawful, vicious lives. Whole families lived by plunder, such as pocket-picking, card-sharping, house-breaking, and almost every other known vice. One family of Irish Cockneys had two sons in penal servitude, and it was three years before the father, and two other sons, could believe that I was what I represented myself to be. The men were seldom to be found at home, as the father went out with what they called the "swag-basket," exchanging china and glass for second-hand clothes; while the sons who lived at home, picked up anything, anywhere. The wife had delicate health, and when I called she would listen to the Word of God. She became anxious about her soul, and was afterwards converted. I was with her when she died.

Looking up at her husband, she said, " Mr. Dunn will look after Bill when he comes home, and will you listen to what he says and promise to meet me in heaven? " Over her remains the husband said, " Now, Mr. Dunn, I believe you are a true man, and want to do us good, but I never did so until now, and there are many others who suspect you."

There were four brothers, named Matthew, Mark, Luke and John, all of whom were believed to be married men, and they were expert gamblers—especially with cards.

When they worked they went as hawkers to houses in well-to-do neighbourhoods. I got intimately acquainted with John, and I trust that both he and his wife became influenced for good, for they used to like to hear the Scriptures read and expounded. The children of these men became experts in everything that was bad and ruinous. The sons were gamblers and thieves, and the daughters became united to men of a similar stamp.

After going round my district several times I began to find out some of the haunts and habits of the people. A great preacher once said :—" The world is my parish." Not so the City Missionary, who has his little plot assigned to him, where he has to devote his time and strength in breaking up the fallow ground, getting out the stones, sowing the seed, and watering it with earnest prayers and tears, and watching for the springing up.

H

There were many discouragements and disappointments, but, thank God, there were some encouragements and blessed compensations. Before I had been at this work twelve months, a clergyman in an adjoining parish had a little talk with me, and expressed his pity for me at having to work in such an awfully degraded spot.

" I've been down here," he said, " for nearly three years, but I cannot stay any longer, for it is like scraping a rock, so I am leaving."

I had to stay, for I knew it was God Who had placed me there, but I dared not leave it until God saw fit to take me away. For ten years I kept on " scraping the rock," and not without some measure of success, graciously granted by God, as the following pages, I trust, will show.

HOW THE POOR LIVE.

The poor among whom I visited appeared to live from hand to mouth, and many lived by plunder. Match-box makers, cobblers—who were nicknamed " translators," because they could turn old boots into new—dust-sifters—who found all kinds of things which were thrown away, and turned them to account—wild-bird catchers for dealers in " Bird Fair " close by, all these were to be found in my district. The men and the women who carried the " swag basket " with china and glass, went into better neighbourhoods to exchange their wares for old clothes, boots, shoes, etc. These were sold to dealers in " the Lane "—a term for Rag

Fair—and the things were then disposed of to " trans- lators " and women who could wash and mend clothes, however bad the things were. They were renovated in a way that would puzzle anyone except the initiated, and were then set out in order, to be sold in the " Fair," where those who were still poorer gathered in hundreds on Sunday mornings. A man could buy a pair of boots for ninepence, another a coat for fifteen pence, another could get a clean-starched shirt for six- pence, another could be seen buying some clean under- garments for a few pence, as those he had on *must* be burnt; a group of women would select dresses, skirts, shawls, or any other article that could be had for a few pence, and mothers would try all sorts of garments on their children.

One thing was very obvious in my visitation in the homes of the very poor, and that was the lack of cup- boards or larders. There appeared to be no place in which to keep their food. I found, however, that they did not need much room, for they usually obtained their food from the little shops as the meal-times came round, and often their meal-times were many hours apart. A remarkable trait was common among the very poorest, and that was the willing way they would share their scanty meal with those who had none.

In the course of my rounds I found many couples living together unmarried, and it was difficult to make them see that it was wrong to live in that state, but as the Word of God was brought to bear on their consciences, some were willing to be married, but others seemed to find it impossible to alter their mode of life, as they had husbands or wives who were living with other people.

EARLY ALLIANCES.

The cause of much of the existing evil and poverty was, no doubt, the early alliances—married or un-married—which frequently took place, when both sexes were in their teens. In order to induce the young people to be married, rather than live together un-married, several ministers of churches performed the marriage service at a reduced fee, while at one or two churches people could be married free of charge. One church in the Bethnal Green Road became very popular on this account, and it was quite a scene on holidays and certain days in the year to see the young people flocking there either to get married or to look on at the ceremony. I have known over twenty young couples meet at that church at one time to be married, and the scenes then and afterwards were so disgraceful that several clergymen agreed not to marry the boys and girls under a certain age, without the written consent of the parents. Notwithstanding the facilities of get-ting married easily, I suppose that where one couple commenced life in this way six couples began living together unmarried.

Another evil among the young people which I noticed during the first few years of my mission work was the very degrading qualifications considered necessary in the case of either youth or maiden. In the case of the former, he must find money to make presents to his girl; to take her frequently to "penny gaffs" (now, happily, rarely to be met with in London); to be a good drinker himself and to supply the girl and her friends with beer; and, above and beyond all, he must be able to fight, so that if anyone offended or insulted her, and she asked him to defend her honour (?), he must be prepared to fight, or be at once discarded. In the case of the latter she must be willing to sing the popular song, dance the usual jig, wear a gaudy frock, and a hat with a big feather in it, so as to attract the attention of the youth above described.

Now to obtain the money necessary to meet these demands was the one great concern with these young folk. Some few might be able to get it by fair means, but many, I found, had to obtain the same by unlawful means. The number of young thieves of both sexes was astounding, and there was a mania for gambling. All these things made my work among the young people most difficult.

PLUNDER AND GAMBLING.

The shortest route for gentlemen walking to the City from the suburbs of Hackney—and the greater number walked in those days—was through Birdcage Walk, Virginia Row, Boundary Street, and out into Shoreditch, and so on. On either side of the route were narrow passages which led into mazes—before referred to—giving every facility for thieves to escape when they secured watches or purses from unwary pedestrians. At certain houses in these places, the "melting pot" was always in readiness to receive valuables if the thief or thieves were hard pressed.

The "light-fingered" gentry were great gamblers, and their ill-gotten spoil would often be gambled away. As many as twenty, thirty, or forty, would sometimes congregate together on Sunday mornings at certain spots in my district for this purpose. "Scouts" were paid to stand at several outposts to give warning of the approach of the police, who mostly went about this neighbourhood in *pairs*.

I became acquainted with the parents of some of these youths, and several were most anxious that I should try and rescue the lads. I made up my mind, that by God's help, I would try to alter these Sabbath morning scenes.

On my first appearance the gamblers scattered like frightened sheep, some of them believing that I was a detective, but I gradually gained their confidence and they would listen for a time while I sang a hymn or read a few verses of Scripture, or had a straight talk with them. The message from God's Word was unto some, I trust, the savour of life unto life, but to others, I fear it was the savour of death unto death. Some of the good people in the neighbourhood were anxious for my personal safety; they most certainly expected that if I did not come to bodily harm I should be set upon and robbed. I continued, however, to warn, entreat, and beseech these gamblers to turn from their sinful ways, with the result that the gang was broken up.

But there was little change in their manner of life. Some, alas, were sent into penal servitude, and one or two were hanged. The father of one youth was much concerned about him, because he spent the greater part of his time in gambling and dancing saloons. He remonstrated with him, saying, "If you go on the way you are going you will be dancing in the air some day." This literally came to pass, for about a year afterwards he was hanged for wilful murder.

HOUSE TO HOUSE.

For about two years I continued to plod on at the work of visitation, often going in and out amidst all kinds of disease, and this told seriously on my health, although I was able to continue at work. Some of the people became impressed, and were converted. I was also able to hold several cottage meetings in different streets and courts, as well as open-air meetings. My old friend Ned came, when he could, to help me. Great commotion was raised in the neighbourhood, and there was, consequently, much opposition.

About this time that fearful scourge of cholera broke out which carried off great numbers. It was a very trying time for visitation. Sometimes I was on my district from morning until far into the night—with

intervals for food and a walk—ministering the Gospel
of mercy to the sick and dying, and beseeching those
who were well to repent and turn to God. Small
depôts with medicines and disinfectants were estab-
lished in different streets and courts, where a doctor
or dispenser was always present to administer them.
Some of the streets and courts were closed as thorough-
fares, and the dead were taken away during the night.
I am thankful to God for preserving me and my family
in health during that fearful time. As I have given a
detailed account of this scourge in my former little
book, "Modern London," I will only add that while
some appeared to be more hardened by this visitation
of cholera, others were seriously impressed by it and
turned to God.

Several of those who were converted became most
anxious to have meetings in their rooms, and so we
held little services in different parts of the district, and
many gathered to hear the Gospel. In fact, so many
came that they could not all get inside, but crowded
round the open door and windows. And the Lord was
present to heal. It was a glad sight to see anxious
souls kneeling around the door, or on the pavement,
pleading for mercy, and someone pointing them to the
"Lamb of God, Which taketh away the sin of the
world."

I must now proceed to give a more detailed account
of my experiences with some typical cases with which
I was graciously permitted to deal.

"FIGHTING BET."

A man and his wife, named D——, lived in a garret in P—— Court, and they both worked in the dustyard. The children ran about the court in filthy rags, while the room presented the appearance of a dust hole, rather than a habitation for human beings. Neither the man nor the woman could read, and their natural inclination led them to drinking, cursing, quarrelling, and fighting. The woman was very powerful, and was often in brawls and fights, hence the name by which she was known—"fighting Bet"—whilst the man was a determined pugilist, and had had nearly every bone in his body broken by fighting, or through accidents when drunk. I could only get a talk with them on Sundays when the wife would be washing or mending the bits of clothing, and the man would often be lying stupidly drunk. There were three children at home, whilst the eldest girl was in the Cripples' Home, having been injured for life by her mother, in a drunken brawl, letting her fall when an infant. Eventually I found an opportunity of bringing the simple truths of the Gospel before the woman, who during an illness was unable to leave the house. It was then that I learnt something of their fearful state. Once after urging her to stop in her mad career before it was too late, she said :—" It's no use me trying to do different while I've got such a —— of a man, but I'd a bin the end of him t'other night, if he'd a come 'ome. I'd got that knife ready, and I'd a given him something for coming in, when I was out, and taking everything he could find for drink, and the money, too, that I'd saved for this job." Some weeks afterwards she went back to the dustyard to work; her child died, and the poor distracted mother was overwhelmed with grief. I tried to comfort her by pointing her to the Lord Jesus, and assuring her that her little lamb was safely folded in His loving arms, but, alas, she flew to the drink, and for awhile so terrible was her career, that it nearly cost her her life. I continued to warn and beseech her to turn to Christ, but could not get her to come to our little meeting.

One evening, however, she passed down the street where we were holding a cottage service, when the singing caused her to stop and listen, but she refused to advance any nearer when the invitation was given by the doorkeeper. She went away, but she came back again shortly afterwards and took a seat just inside the door, and in that little room the Holy Spirit used His own sword to lay bare her heart, and to convince her of her lost state. From that time she evidenced a sincere desire to flee from the wrath to come, but it was some time before she could realize her acceptance with God. At length the light broke in, and she was made really happy, and then to see her, early or late, whenever and wherever she could hear the Word of Life, and learn about her Saviour, always thirsting for the Water of Life, was, indeed, a grand contrast to what we had known of her former life.

She now became anxious about her husband, who would have nothing to do with religion, but plunged deeper into all kinds of wickedness, and the poor woman's trials and temptations were very great, for she not only had her husband and children to contend with at home, but nearly every youth and girl in the dustyard wanted to fight her. "Yes, Sir," she said one day, "to be cursed and jeered at and challenged to fight by these young folks in the yard, who a short time ago dared not lift a finger to me, is one of the hardest trials I have to bear. I must bear it, however, until it pleases God to take me out of it, which I pray He will do when He sees fit."

About this time her husband had the misfortune to break his leg, while fighting with another man, and was taken to the hospital. His wife visited him and talked to him about his soul as well as she could, and one day he sent word by her that he would like to see me. I went and found him in a serious mood, and apparently prepared to receive instruction. He was deeply moved while listening to the story of the Cross, and with tears in his eyes, he said, "If I come out you will see me a far different man from what I used to be." After being in the hospital some months he was sent out, a cripple for life, but was able to get about with the aid of crutches. He used to come to the meetings, and with the spirit of a child would sit and learn the A B C of religion, while the people who had known him for years could only wonder. One day, he said, "I'm afraid it's too much to believe that God has fully forgiven me, such a sinner as I've been."

As the man was unable to work, the wife had to support them by her industry as well as she could. Sometimes they were in deep poverty, but she cheerfully said, "I would rather be like this than have plenty of money and live in sin." Speaking one day about the mercy of God, she exclaimed, "When I think of what I've been, and what I've done, I can see nothing but the mercy of God. Why, sir, I've hurled those sharp knives across the room at my children in the height of passion, and sometimes they have stuck fast in that wood. Had it not missed them it must surely have caused their death. However they escaped I cannot tell. I've waited for my husband coming upstairs, with a knife concealed, determined to strike a fatal blow, but he didn't come. We've fought with deadly weapons, in fact, it's the greatest mercy in the world that we have not both been hanged on the gallows."

In course of time she learnt to read a little; and, as she was very strong, she secured some good places as charwoman, and so was able to leave the dustyard. In the evenings and on days when she was not at work she would attend to poor sick women and children in the district, and when anyone was taken very ill usually the first thing that was said was "Send for Mrs. D——," no longer "fighting Bet." A friend of the Mission came to see the district, and after observing the condition in which many of the poor women and children were in, she offered to support a nurse if one could be found. Mrs. D—— accepted the post, which she filled satisfactorily for some time. Her husband—as we have said—was crippled for life, but she kept him as long as he lived. She ultimately obtained a good situation as nurse in an Institution, and, whenever she could get out, she would come over to see us, and attend a meeting at the Mission Room, which in course of time we obtained. On one occasion when she came in, a local tradesman, who had known her well in the old days, was giving an address. At its close he asked me who that lady-like person was. I told him, and he was astounded. "What! do you mean to say that is 'Fighting Bet'? I can scarcely believe it, and yet it is, sure enough. Well, I should have almost as soon have expected to have seen Satan himself changed as that woman, and yet there she is."

As I contemplate the awful condition in which this woman and her husband were when I first met them, and what, by the grace of God, they became, I can only exclaim, "Is anything too hard for the Lord?"

IN WORKSHOPS.

There were about fifty workshops—large and small—with over two hundred men at work, and these I visited in order. During the first twelve months I had a rough time with most of the men, being received with coarse ribaldry and not a little rough usage. I was never seriously injured, but was sometimes warned as to what would happen if I ever came again. Yet I never shrank from going, and if any of them became very desperate I appealed to them, as a man who had not just come out of a "band box," but who had seen more of the world and of working men than some of them. At the same time I conceded that if they were all agreed that I should not visit them I would consider their decision. I never found a shop where they were all so agreed, for there were always some who were glad to hear what I had to say, and would receive tracts and other good literature.

There were a few rather clever infidels among these men, for about this time Charles Bradlaugh had great influence, yet I found that they did not like me to use my Bible in dealing with their arguments. Often did they say, "Put up that Book and argue without it," but my reply was, "No, this is the highest authority we have, and from this there is no appeal." I always used the Word for the defence of the Gospel, and also for real aggressive work, being convinced that that was the great instrument in the hands of the Holy Spirit for bringing a rebel back to God.

There were others who rejected the Bible and religion because, having been brought up without them, they did not want to trouble about them now.

"I like to see you come here, and to hear you talk," said a man one day, "but I shall not let you come and see me when I'm dying, as you did old S——, for he preached away to his son after that, and told him he had found out that he had been wrong and begged him to stop drinking and swearing before it was too late. No, Sir, my old father would not let a parson come to talk and pray with him when he was dying, and I will not.''

'' Well,'' I replied, '' if you should be called to die, and you will send for me, or if I should know of it, I will try and come and pray with you.''

The drinking habits and late hours of this man told upon him, and in less than twelve months his wife came and told me she believed he was dying, and that he would like to see me. I went to his room. He grasped my hand, and I at once pointed him to the Saviour. He could not talk much, but I read the Scriptures and prayed with him. Before I called again he had passed away. His determined hostility had certainly broken down, and his wife said, '' He seemed to be praying when he died.''

BITTER OPPOSITION GIVING WAY.

The results of several such deaths and the continual visitation by the missionary, had a somewhat subduing effect on the workmen in the shops. Swearing and jeering began to give way before earnest prayer and patient perseverance. In time no more welcome visitor than the missionary entered the shop, and the parish clergyman, who was my local superintendent, and sometimes accompanied me, would express his astonishment at the way in which they received me, and listened to a word of warning or exhortation.

"No clergyman," he said, "could have effected such a change in so short a time, but, as a man among men, and one well acquainted with their prejudices and customs, the City Missionary can accomplish much."

"WHERE IS THIS TEXT?"

One day I entered a cabinet-making shop, where I found some fresh men at work. To see me come in with my Book was an opportunity for them to have some fun, for they were on "piece work." After some pleasant banter and chaff about my being ignorant of working men, and not being acquainted with the questions of the day, like Charles Bradlaugh, they hinted that I might be better employed than by wasting my time with them. I answered a few of their questions and told them that I knew something about working men, and that I had learnt a few things which had been most helpful to me, and which I was anxious to make known to others.

While I was speaking thus, I saw a consultation going on between several of them, and soon one bright-looking fellow came up to me, and pointing to the Bible that was in my hand, said, "What book is that?" "It is the Bible," I replied. "Do you teach that?" he asked. "Oh, yes," I said. "Then will you tell me where this text is to be found, 'Out of him came forth the corner, out of him the nail, out of him the battle-bow, out of him every oppressor together'?" I opened my Bible and read to them the fourth verse of the tenth chapter of Zechariah, being the text asked for. The man, turning to his shopmates—some of whom had been plying their infidel questions—said, "Now, mates, I have one thing to say, and it is this, whenever this gentleman comes to see you, listen to what he has to say, for whatever you may think he does not know, I can tell you he knows his Book."

The men went back to their benches to work, but I told their spokesman that I must have another word with him, to which he agreed.

"I think you know something more about the good old Book than just that text, do you not?"

"Yes, I ought to, for my parents read it, and I was taught to read it in our home in the country. In fact I could pass a fair examination on it now."

I then told him a little of my own experience, how for years I had neglected to read my Bible, and the remarkable way in which God brought me back to it, and I urged him to seek to know Christ as his Saviour through the Scriptures. He listened, and admitted that he ought to attend to these things.

A remarkable change came over the bulk of the men in these workshops. Some, I am thankful to say, were converted to God, and became witnesses for Him, others were outwardly reformed, and led better lives, while those who adhered to their drinking, vicious ways, did not go to such lengths as formerly.

A gentleman was going round the district with me one day, and was remarking on the squalor and wretchedness to be seen on every hand, when the employer of a number of men in cabinet-making came by, and entered into conversation with me. I introduced the gentleman as one who took a great interest in seeking to uplift the people.

"Yes," he said, "I do take a great interest in them, but the people around here seem to be in a very sunken condition, and the public-houses seem to be thronged with working men. Do you not think the missionary had better go somewhere else and try what he can do?"

"I hope the missionary will not be taken away from us," the employer replied, "for Heaven knows the men are bad enough now, but what sort of demons they would be if he did not come among them sometimes, I cannot tell. He has a far greater influence over my men than I have, and can get them in to work when I am quite unable to do so. It is not long since I had a very special order in hand, and it had to be delivered by a certain time. Well, Monday, Tuesday and Wednesday passed, and I could not get them from the public-house. On Thursday morning I was distracted, when I happened to meet the missionary, and asked him if he could help me. He said, 'I'll try,' and he went to the public-house, and, in less than half an hour, brought the bulk of the men to work; the rest soon followed, and I was able to deliver the order. Yes, Sir, we indeed need a missionary in this neighbourhood to help to keep the men a bit square."

EFFORTS IN THE OPEN-AIR.

Soon after commencing my work here I began to preach in the open-air, and, as I have said, my friend Ned often came over to help me. In addition to speaking in every street and court in the district, we held meetings on Sundays and certain week-nights, in front of the disused chapel, opening out of the Bethnal Green Road, and also on a piece of waste ground in front of the then notorious "Bird Cage" public-house, near to Columbia Market. We met with great opposition the first summer, and this continued more or less for several seasons. We felt, at times, almost disposed to surrender to the enemy, but our efforts were sustained by a few saintly praying women, whom my dear wife gathered together once a week to plead with God in prayer on our behalf.

The first spot referred to was well situated for getting at the throngs of men on Sunday mornings, on their way to the noted Bird Fair not far away. Yet such was the bitterness of some bigoted Romanists, and scoffing infidels, that they would throw refuse and offal at us, and even come close to us while speaking and strike brimstone matches under our noses; in fact, they would use all kinds of offensive and mean acts to try and stop us. Still we persevered, and ultimately God gave us the victory.

A young infidel lived with his parents in a street near by. He secured the help of others, together with several lecturers and debaters from the (so-called) "Hall of Science," and the scenes on Sunday were truly awful. I deemed it best to preach the Gospel on that spot on Sunday afternoons or evenings, while this infidel rowdyism was going on. Perhaps I cannot do better than give a letter which appeared in a Christian paper from the pen of a gentleman, who was connected with the "Bible Defence Association" :—

"Infidels in Bethnal Green."

"Among the natives of Bethnal Green parish, I understand that Mr. ————, the Apostle of Atheism, is one. A few weeks back some of that individual's admirers and followers commenced Sunday morning lectures, with discussions, in Bethnal Green. In consequence of communications received by me, I went last Sunday morning and found a young man haranguing a crowd in a fluent and flippant style. He was one of a company of young men who actively endeavour to promulgate hostility to all religion. Their unprincipled lying, and bitter malice, have often been exposed by myself and friends in different places. The audience, I am loth to describe. Go through London and you will scarcely be able to find any hundred and fifty men and boys whose appearance is better fitted to fill the friends of humanity with grim despair. If any one is really anxious to know what low types of humanity remain in Bethnal Green, after all that

Miss Coutts has done, let him go to Gibraltar Walk on Sunday at noon. I protested against a mischievous falsehood which the lecturer had uttered and the consequence was a scene of confusion, which indicated the dominant spirit of the crowd. Consequently I tried to speak, but the moment I began I was stopped by the yells and howls of the fellow-parishioners of Mr. Bradlaugh. We made known, as best we could, the Way of Life, and urged men to stop their clamour and think. Many tracts were given away, and we showed that the followers of Christ can advocate His Gospel even amid ravening wolves. This was much, but we learned some lessons. The ruffian infidelity at certain centres of N. and N.-W. London is a thing of the past, but here, in Bethnal Green, brutal approbation of unbelief, and lies, and maliciousness, start up suddenly in stalwart proportions. What we heard last Sunday is not fitted to civilize the savages of this locality. The Gospel alone will do that."

I continued to hold meetings on that spot, and by speech and song proclaimed God's great love for poor lost sinners in the gift of Jesus Christ. On many occasions some infidels were present, and would taunt and jeer, especially at my wife and others, while they were giving away tracts, or speaking to the people. These opponents urged the people not to read them, and they boasted at *their* meeting that they would have such an organization as would be able to stop all the open-air preaching in East London. But we had unseen forces of which they knew nothing. Our little band of prayer-helpers kept on at their work, while men—some of whom had been notorious characters in the neighbourhood—and women, who had been converted to God through visitation, came to the meetings as witnesses to the saving power of the Gospel. It was a wonderful sight to see numbers of bird-fanciers, with little cages under their arms—the confined songsters trilling their sweet melodies, as we were singing for Jesus—stand, with pipes in their hands, looking aghast at some of their number who were singing with us instead of accompanying them to the Bird Fair. Such witnesses did more to destroy the effects of infidel propaganda than debates and arguments. Then, also, one of the principal speakers among the infidels—a young man of fairly good education, and who was thought much of by the fraternity—became converted, and this was to them a staggering blow. It came about in this way.

This young man not only attended infidel meetings to speak or debate, but when he found what gatherings we had he came with a Saul-like determination to make havoc of us. One Sunday, after he had been speaking indignantly against the Bible, and those who believed in it, my wife got him a little away from our gathering and talked to him in such a way, pleading with him as a young man of education to read, and think about his position, that he said, '' Well, I've never been talked to in this fashion, and by a woman, too. You must not think that you are going to convert me, for I could never believe the Bible.'' '' Well, you read it,'' she said, '' and I will pray for you, and you may yet be-

come a preacher of the truths you now denounce."
"That's quite enough for you this time," he said, and
went away.

It would occupy too much space to narrate in detail
the course of this young man's life, but it may be said
that he ultimately became converted, was denounced by
the infidel party, was taken in hand by a clergyman
whom I knew, was eventually ordained, and became a
minister of that blessed Gospel that he once sought to
destroy.

> "God moves in a mysterious way,
>   His wonders to perform."

The boast of the infidel party that they would stop
open-air preaching in the whole of East London came
to naught; the Sunday morning scenes at their meetings were stopped, we were left in peaceful possession,
and a blessed work for God was carried on.

The bitter opposition and strife—almost heartbreak-
ing—which we endured for several seasons redounded
to the glory of God in many ways. The people of the
district who had been won for Christ were very anxious
to have a Mission Room, as a centre from which to
carry on operations for the Master, and special prayer
was offered that God would open the way. Several
Christian tradesmen in the neighbourhood were con-
sulted, amongst them Mr. W. Fox—a wholesale and
retail chemist, and also a Guardian of the poor. He
said, "Yes, I shall be most happy to assist in supporting a Mission Room, for as my wife and I, on our

way to Church, have seen the bitter opposition to your open-air work, and how you have stuck to your post, I have often said to her, 'Yon man has some grit to stand what he has to do, and if he ever wants help, I'll give it.'"

In due course a place was secured, and fitted up as a Mission Room, and most blessed work was carried on there for the benefit of the poor.

" THE BIRD CAGE."

This was a public-house at the northern corner of my district, and near to Columbia Square and Market, which did a tremendous business. There was also one at another corner nearly opposite, "The Virginia Planter," which was reputed to be in as flourishing a condition. There were five roads converging to this point, and the two main positions were occupied by these two houses. When I first began work in the district the rent collector of some slum property said that the landlord of the "Bird Cage" had refused eighteen thousand pounds for the good-will of the house, but that the "Virginia Planter" could be had for fifteen or sixteen thousand.

As I have said, it was on a piece of waste ground where a number of old houses had been cleared away, in front of these two houses, that we held meetings, and wonderful times we had. Several once notorious customers at the "Bird Cage" became converted to God, and in course of time were bold witnesses to the power of the Gospel. From that time the tremendous influence of the " Bird Cage " began to wane.

A gentleman when going by the house with me one night, and hearing the hilarious singing and shouting at a free and easy concert, said :—

" Now, friend, if you can shut up a few of these places I should say that you missionaries were doing something to better the neighbourhood."

" I'm afraid we cannot do that," I replied, " but we can try and help some who are willing to be rescued from the downward path to ruin."

" But," he asked, " do you mean to say that you get any out of that place ? "

" Yes," I replied, " and if you will come to our Mission Room just down that street on Sunday evening you will see four men singing for Jesus, who were once the principal singers in that house."

SOME ROUGH DIAMONDS.

Under this heading I will briefly describe some of the men who were rescued and saved from the sin and degradation in which they were found in this noted public-house. I will only give their initials for obvious reasons, and relate the cases for the glory of God.

I.

J. C—— was a man much sought after. He was a good singer ; a great sportsman in managing bird-singing matches, rat-killing matches, dog fights, and cockfights, and a desperate pugilist. In all these kinds of sport he had practised cruelty which we will not attempt to describe. When he became converted it caused a tremendous commotion in the various houses in which he was known. By trade he was a shoemaker, but it was very little time he could spare for honest toil.

I had often dealt with him in his own room, but he was always more ready to talk about his dogs, or birds, with which his room was stored, than about the way of Life. At length the Bible, which I had persuaded him to read, awakened his conscience, and, the truths being applied by the Holy Spirit, resulted in a full surrender of himself and all he had to God. He now became as zealous in God's work as he was before in Satan's service. He delighted to stand in the open-air and sing for Jesus, and he threw his whole soul into all the work in connection with the Mission Room. He was a great power at our prayer meetings, and he never prayed without being melted into tears. I asked him once why he wept so when he prayed.

"Oh, Sir," he replied, " I know that God has forgiven me, but when I pray, and think what a sinful wretch I've been, and what I've done against such a loving Father, I cannot help but weep." He got together a band of twelve for the purpose of distributing tracts on Sunday afternoons. He was made Secretary, and they called him their Captain. They had printed covers for the tracts stating the name and place of the

Mission Room, and the time of the various meetings. We always met for prayer before they started on their much-loved work, and the first Sunday was one of intense interest. Our good friend had sketched out the districts, and about 25 houses were allotted to each worker, my wife taking one. When each knew where his little field was, J. C—— was asked what part he was going to take. He replied, " I'm going to take the court where I lived my wicked life for so many years, and where I now want to live and witness for Jesus."

He continued to do this work for some years, and the influence he exerted in the place was marvellous. One Sunday, when I was visiting some very serious cases of illness, and was about to enter a room in the court, I heard the voice of J—— earnestly praying with the sick man. I did not enter that sacred spot, but my heart was overwhelmed with joy, as I thought of past days, when these two men had met each other in the prize-fighting ring, and the last encounter was so terrible that it was thought that the one then on his sickbed was killed. Now they were meeting for the last time on earth, not to fight each other ; no, for while one was engaged in " the last combat," the other was pleading with God in his behalf, and pointing him to " the Lamb of God Which taketh away the sin of the world."

Thus he continued to witness for his Master till he was called to higher service. His dying request was, that as they carried his mortal remains out of the court, his comrades in the Lord's work would sing his favourite hymn in front of the coffin :—

" Safe in the arms of Jesus."

II.

W. M—— was a young married man, with two young children, when I first met him. He was a fancy-slipper maker, but he worked very little at his trade, as the " Bird Cage " was his principal centre of attraction. He was a good comic singer, and was in great demand. Sometimes during the holiday season he was away from home two or three weeks at a time, with a nigger troupe. He would earn a good sum in this way, but it did not benefit his home at all, for it all went in drink.

His parents lived next door to the Church, but they never went inside. The father was proud of his boy, and trained him, at the age of nine years, to become a " star," by taking him to the " Bird Cage," and showing the company how much beer the lad could drink out of a quart pot. He would then put him on a barrel to sing a lewd song. So he grew up, never going to school, but became an expert in everything that was degrading and vile.

He had to keep moving about from place to place when he got married, because he would pay no rent if he could avoid it. He came under our notice in the following way :—

One Sunday afternoon a tract distributer knocked at the door of a little room in her district, when a young woman opened it, and being too deaf to hear what was said, she roused her husband, who was in a drunken sleep in one corner of the room. " Bill," she shouted, " wake up, you're wanted." Seeing a tall young lady in the room he was greatly surprised, and at length he asked her what she wanted. " Will you read a little book I've brought you? " " Can't read," he replied. " Well, shall I read a little to you? " she asked. " If you like," he answered. She read a few verses from the Testament and offered a short prayer, simply asking God to bless them. She called the next night, and again read and prayed with them. He never forgot that prayer.

The visitor, after telling me about her calls, asked me to see them. I found the man at home, but, oh ! what a place to call home. Bare walls, not an article of furniture, a few rags in one corner, and two little children who (it will scarcely be believed) were quite naked. The woman wore an old skirt, while the man had on a black coat buttoned close up to the neck, for he had no shirt to wear. He said he was sorry he couldn't ask me to sit down as he had nothing in the place but that old box. Still I sat on that, and after having a chat, I ventured to ask him what he thought of religion.

" I don't know anything about that," he replied, " but I've been thinking that the way I've been going on all my life has never done me any good. Why, I never heard anyone ask God to bless me and my little family, until that young lady did, and I can't forget it."

I read a part of the Epistle to the Romans, showing man's state by nature, and the way of Life through Christ, and prayed with him. He asked me to call again. The following Sunday evening he came to the meeting, and I could see that the Holy Spirit was working powerfully within him. He was very attentive, and his tears flowed copiously through the whole of the service, at the close of which I urged him to trust wholly in the Saviour. But, oh! how dark his mind was. I called on him in the week and found him at work.

"I've felt most wretched since Sunday night," he said, "for all that you said condemned me; yet I remember you said something about a Man Who would receive whosoever came to Him, and I've been wondering if He would take me, for you said, that *whosoever* meant everyone in the world. I wonder if He would have anything to do with me, for I don't mind telling you, Sir, but it is a wonder I've not been led to the gallows, like some of my old pals have."

I told him the Person I had been speaking of, Who would receive all who came to Him, was the Lord Jesus Christ.

"Where is He, then?" he asked.

"In Heaven," I replied.

"Then," said he, looking amazed, "how can a poor fellow like me go to Him?"

Such was the darkness and the ignorance through which the poor fellow was groping his way. I sought to lead him gradually into the Light, and at length he was led by the Spirit to full Salvation. The simple knowledge that Christ loved him, and was able to save him, won his heart completely.

How anxious he was to learn more of these things, but he met with much opposition, and, as he could not read he could not meet the infidel objections to the Bible. Yet he would say, "Come to the Mission Room and hear for yourself," and some did come.

A Christian gentleman offered to teach those who could not read or write, twice a week, and this poor man, among others, accepted the offer. He made rapid progress, for the instructor, who had been a Moravian missionary, was a wonderful teacher, and W. M—— soon became able to read some of the lessons from a book published by the "Sunday School Union" for teaching adults to read. Calling to see him one day, he said, "Oh, Mr. Dunn, look here, I've been reading lesson XV. in my book, and it is so beautiful that I asked my wife to read it to me again, as she can read better than I can. It's the best I've read, and I mean to keep it. He began to read it to me, 'The Lord is my Shepherd, I shall not want.'" I procured him a Bible, which was his daily companion, and he was soon able to read some parts of the New Testament intelligently.

The change of heart was manifest in his life, and his wife and friends could not make it out. He was often sought after by his old associates, among whom were "light-fingered gentry," "niggers," "penny gaff" singers, dancers, and others, for Bill was an adept in all these arts and crafts. He thought of several plans by which to meet them, but the most effectual one was repeating two texts he had learnt :— (1) "If any man be in Christ, he is a new creature; old things are passed away : behold all things are become new." (2) "The blood of Jesus Christ, His Son, cleanseth us from all sin."

He settled down to honest toil, and as he was considered a good workman, and could give security, he was able to get a superior class of work from the warehouse. After taking his work in he returned home with the whole of his earnings, which he deposited on the little box in front of his wife. She looked at it in amazement and said, "Bill, where have you been, have you met anybody?" "It's all right, gal," he shouted, "take it up, it's all yours." She did so with mingled feelings of fear and joy.

Clothes for themselves and children were soon purchased, and also furniture for their room. Some time after he said to his wife, "I say, gal, I've heard folks say that time is money, and I'm often behind at the meetings, what say you, shall we have a clock?" She

NEW CLOCK IN A SLUM.

consented, and he started off to a shop in Shoreditch. After looking round the place and asking the price of several, he selected one, about the biggest dial in the shop, possibly thinking the biggest must be the best. Putting down the price, he packed up and started for home. His wife and children looked on with intense interest while the big nail was driven into the wall and the clock adjusted. When it was in working order, and began to strike, the children could contain themselves no longer, but began to dance, as they were in the habit of doing when the barrel-organ began to play, and the elder one shouted, " Dadda's brought a talker home! " No wonder, for the little things had never seen a clock before.

Things kept on improving with them until they got Sunday clothes, and it was a glad sight to see them all march in their Sunday best to the tea and public meeting just then being held. Walking up to me with his children, he looked at them as much as to say, " What do you think of them now? " One friend remarked, " Why, W. M—— is quite a gentleman, he has tidy clothes on, new boots, a white shirt and necktie, in fact, he is not the same man he was when he first came to the Mission Room."

Emissaries were often sent out from the " Bird Cage " to try and persuade Bill to come and sing, but he always met their persuasions with his texts. They now turned on his father, who still frequented the house, and taunted him with allowing Bill to be led

K

away by religious shams, after bringing him up so carefully. The father, feeling desperate, threatened to be the death of the missionary, if he could only get the chance, and one night he came to the Hall with his pocket full of stones, for the purpose of inflicting an injury.

W. M—— became most anxious about his parents, and brothers and sisters, and did all he could to get them to the Mission Hall. One Sunday evening he had the joy of bringing his parents and sisters, and they listened most attentively. I spoke to them at the close, and the father trembled and wept, and while I shook his hand he sobbed out, "I hope you will forgive me for what I've said about you, Sir." "You have done no harm to me," I replied, "you must ask God to forgive you." When they got home he said, "Bill, I never heard anything like that, and the missionary is quite a different man from what I thought. I've never been into any place of worship since I went to Church to be married till to-night, but I mean to go again."

On another occasion our friend brought his parents and brothers, as well as some rough-looking companions of former days from the "Bird Cage," and God gave us a good time. It was a wonderful sight to see Bill—while all were on their knees in the prayer meeting—praying, weeping, and pleading with them to give their hearts to God.

On yet another occasion he brought sixteen men out

of the "Bird Cage" to the service, several of whom were won for Christ, and at the close of the meeting his face shone with joy, as he exclaimed, "If God will give me more grace and knowledge we will shake the 'Bird Cage' all to pieces yet."

III.

H. K—— was also a young married man with two children, and being a shoe-maker by trade was known to our friend W. M——, who was, in fact, the means of bringing him to the Mission Room. The Word was applied by the Holy Ghost with power to the heart and conscience of this man, and for some time he laboured under deep conviction, but at length, by simple faith, he was made happy in the love of Christ.

This man's conversion caused a great uproar, not only among his own relations—who, it was said, numbered nearly two hundred—but among his pals, for if W. M—— was their star, H. K—— was a great leader, and they were determined to get him back again, or they would kick up a big row, so they said. Poor H. K—— trembled when he heard this, and when he saw them enter the Hall he wondered how it would end.

Strange to say they remained quiet the whole time, and went away orderly, but a cousin of his said, "We must have a lot of drink before we go again." They came again, and some of them were the worse for drink, but there was no disturbance. Sometimes a fresh lot of his old companions would come to see for themselves, so they said, and to hear H. K—— pray. The latter asked one of them, who was a determined sceptical opponent, what he thought of the service. "Oh," he said, "I did not know how to sit, I could compare it to nothing else but like throwing bricks at your head." He continued to come and became truly anxious about his soul.

H. K——'s eldest brother had been an ardent follower of Mr. Bradlaugh for ten years, and boasted that he had burnt three Bibles, and did not care for any parson or missionary. One night he came, and, with a defiant air, took a seat in the middle of the Hall, with his hat on, which, however, he was induced to remove. He sat with head erect, his eyes fixed in a determined way on a corner of the ceiling, but towards the close, as H. K—— was praying, he presented a different attitude. Great surprise was manifested when on the following Sunday he again walked in and took a seat, with a little more reverence. The third time he came he joined in the singing, and when prayer was offered he bowed his head. He left off going to infidel meetings, his children were sent to Sunday School, and his wife attended the Mothers' Meeting, where they were taught, by my wife, to cut out and make garments for their children.

In course of time H. K—— became very useful as an open-air speaker, and when he mounted the little stand on the waste ground in front of the "Bird

PREACHING TO THE CROWD.

Cage," the customers would stream out of the two houses to hear his thrilling experience, and to hear their old companion sing. "Now, mates," he would say, "you all know me, and you all know what I was in the past, and you see what I am now. You know how several homes have gone for drink while my wife and children wanted bread, and I have not had clothes or boots fit to wear. Yes, you know all this, and a great deal more, and you see me now the same man, and yet not the same, but a new man in Christ Jesus, and do you want to know how it came about? Now, listen, and I will tell you."

Then, with pipes taken out of their mouths, and eyes fixed on him, they would listen to the story of his conversion, and of Christ, the Mighty to save.

Signs were not wanting to show how the power of the Holy Spirit was at work among the people gathered there. The earnest look on the faces, and the orderly crowd, were all evidences that the speaker had gained his point, and he was driving it home to the hearts of the people by the power of God, backed by the prayers of the faithful few—the little working band of Christians.

Through the influence of H. K—— and his companion Bill, the "Bird Cage" began to lose many of its customers. The landlord became desperate when he saw his takings gradually diminishing, and his business doomed to destruction. He called on several local tradesmen and said he should no longer deal with them, as he knew they "encouraged the missionary and his gang."

IV.

Among many who were saved from these houses I will only refer to one more, which completes the " four men singing for Jesus " before referred to.

This man's name was H. D——, and he possessed the best voice of the four. He was very regular at the " Bird Cage," and could always get plenty of encores. He worked in a hearth-rug weaving shop, and was a man deep dyed in sin. His master said to me, " Don't mind about the rest of the men, Sir, but look after H. D——, for it is time he altered, or I do not know what the end will be."

He had a Godly brother who was a blacksmith, and when he heard that I was visiting H. D—— in the shop and at his home, he said,

" Now I believe my brother will be saved and delivered from his drinking and song-singing in the ' Cage.' You keep bringing before him the Word of God, and his own sinful life, while I continue to pray for him."

For a time H. D—— fought against all reasoning and truth, and at last he would go away when he saw me, determined to have nothing to do with me, or my teaching.

I sometimes felt I must relinquish my efforts, when he resented them so bitterly, but his brother urged me to persevere. We did persevere, and after a while I found that H. D—— was being terribly shaken, for at times he could neither work, sleep, nor take part in the concert room.

This sort of thing increased considerably until his shopmates said he was going "daft." His brother was gladdened by the signs, and felt persuaded that the "New Birth" was near. H. D——'s wife now became seriously alarmed at his state of mind, and told her neighbours that she must leave him as he was much worse than when he used to get drunk.

The crisis was reached one morning when his wife sent for me saying, that as I was the cause of his being in such a state, I must look after him, or have him removed, for she dared not stop with him another night.

"Last night," she said, "he kept jumping out of bed, and falling on the floor, crying out to God to have mercy on him. I had no rest, and can endure it no longer."

The man sat in a most distressed and exhausted condition, for his poor broken heart and bruised spirit were just ready for the healing balm of the Gospel, and I had only to deal it out from the Word of God to a soul most anxious for it. After a time the clouds began to disperse, and light came. Falling on his knees he asked me to pray, and while I was doing so he started to sing, and the wife, in a most excited state, said she was sure he was going to die. I assured her that he was just beginning to live, and that she would have a better husband after this.

He felt better after a night's rest, and was able to resume his work, fortified and strengthened for the ridicule and persecution it was his lot to bear for many days to come. He had the help and encouragement of a Godly brother, and all the inducement of his old companions and the landlord to get him to pay another visit to the " Cage " were unavailing. He had left it for ever.

Thus the " Bird Cage " received a severe shaking, and as far as I know it never recovered from the shock.

HARVESTING.

After several years of hard toil in breaking up the fallow ground, and a period of patient seed-sowing which, God knows, was many a night watered with prayers and tears, I had, before the end of this decade, the great joy of harvest—of bringing in the sheaves, for which God be praised. A wave of blessing, or saving grace, went over this sin-stricken neighbourhood, and many were converted. Some account of the cases has been given in my little book, " Modern London," but it would require another volume to record them all.

OLD JOE.

I must, however, just give one more case, as it resulted in much service for the Master.

A man and his wife—both sixty years of age—named Whiting, lived in Princes Court, and one of their sons, a shoemaker, lived with them. When I first met them I found the wife loved and read her Bible, and was a quiet Christian, but her husband was altogether opposed to the Gospel. I would often talk with him about salvation, but he appeared to get worse, and so his wife and I agreed to unite in special prayer in his behalf. At length his wife came to the meeting, and with joy beaming in her eyes, said, '' I can see a little cloud arising, come and see him as soon as you can.'' I went to see him and there he sat with his head buried in his hands. I laid my hand on his shoulder and asked that all-important question, '' What do you think about the salvation of your soul?'' He looked up for a second, and burying his face again in his hands, while tears blinded his eyes, he exclaimed, '' Oh, Sir, I'm lost, I'm lost!'' He sat there, rocking to and fro and groaning bitterly, crying out, '' I'm lost, I'm going to hell, oh, what shall I do?'' When he became a little calmer, I pointed him to Christ, and assured him that '' He came to seek and to save that which was lost,'' and quoted some precious invitations. '' That's true,'' he cried, '' but there is no mercy for me. It's too far gone. You don't know what a wretch I've been. I, sixty years a sinner, and guilty of all kinds of sin and crime.'' Here he wrung his hands in bitter anguish.

This agony continued for more than an hour, until

he was quite prostrate, and he fell back, as though he were about to die, the perspiration pouring from him. I tried to lead him from Sinai to Calvary, telling him that his Deliverer was *there*. I sympathized with him, having passed through the same struggle, and told him how the Lord delivered me.

"Do you think there is mercy for me?" he cried.

"Yes, for the vilest sinner," I replied.

Then falling on his knees he said, "Pray for me." I knelt by his side, and his wife in one corner of the room bowed her head in prayer. Rising from our knees, he exclaimed, "I see a little light." I exhorted him to keep looking to Christ on the cross, and pray for the Holy Spirit. I left him with the words, "Him that cometh to Me, I will in *no* wise cast out."

For several days after he seemed to be struggling between hope and fear, but at length the light from Heaven flooded his soul, and he could rejoice in Christ as his salvation. He told me that the first thing which disturbed his mind was the thought of being eternally separated from his wife.

He grew in grace, had an ardent love for the Saviour and became zealous in good works. He helped us considerably in the open-air meetings, much to the astonishment of the neighbours, who exclaimed, "Just look at 'Old Joe,' who'd believe it was him!"

About twelve months after this a lady from the Isle of Wight, who took a great interest in the London City Mission, visited the district, and calling upon my superintendent—the Clergyman—found out from him that what was needed was a Bible woman, to teach and help the poor women. This lady offered to support one if a suitable woman could be found. Several women offered themselves, among them being Mrs. Whiting. Her knowledge of the Scriptures was so extensive that she was at once chosen to fill that post. The good she did was inestimable, and she was designated the "walking Bible," for whatever conversation the women were engaged in she would answer them, or turn the drift of their conversation by the Word of God.

The following winter a man was required to make soup for the starving poor, and "Old Joe" was chosen, and they removed to rooms on the school premises.

They were both very happy in their work, and God blessed their labours, while their gratitude to God was abounding. "Years ago," he said, "I had a nice little fortune left me, when in Suffolk, but I spent it all in drink and sinful pleasure, and when I think of the abounding grace of God in saving my soul from destruction, yes, and also in saving us from the workhouse, my heart overflows."

In course of time he fell ill, and it was apparent that he was about to die. Just before the end came, he said, "I think I am going, but it's all right, Jesus is mine, and I am His." His dear wife repeated some precious promises to him, and looking at her, he said, "I've got it, 'I will——never——leave—'" He could say no more, but his wife finished the sentence and he nodded assent. These were his last words. He passed away very peacefully—a brand plucked from the fire.

Some time after his death the widow had to give up her much loved work, and went to end her days in the village where she was born.

A REPORT AND AN APPEAL.

Towards the end of this period our good Secretary published an account of the work in the Society's Magazine, and made a strong appeal for funds in order that more missionaries might be placed in the " moral wastes " around this district.

At the same time I was called upon to attend public meetings, both in London and the provinces, and tell of the work that had been done, and was being carried on in this district. Many became deeply interested in the work of the Society, and some who had means had their sympathies stirred to render substantial help. There were others who doubted the awful picture drawn by the report in the Magazine and the statements made at public meetings. Many either came themselves or sent deputies to investigate the condition of things. On three sides of my district there were no missionaries for some distance, and I was often asked to visit some desperate case, for the places and the characters of the people were about as bad as my own district. Pressmen were also sent to investigate the state of the neighbourhood and to make their own reports for the public. To show the reader that the description I have given is not overdrawn I will give a few extracts from a daily paper, describing the district after I had been at work in it about nine years.

THE NEIGHBOURHOOD AS SEEN BY AN OUTSIDER.

"Go through Columbia Square and all you will see bears an air of respectability. Cross the street and the reverse picture strikes you with equal force. There are little two-storied houses shaking with age or dilapidation. The windows look as if they had never been cleaned for a generation, many of them are broken, the broken panes being supplied by sheets of dirty paper or dirtier rags. The doors are crowded by women and children who seem to have an irrepressible aversion to soap and water. The women are slatternly, the children run about in tatters; decency and these people are no friends. Entering one house I found a family consisting of father and mother and five children living in one little room called a parlour. The room in which the cooking was done, in which the seven human beings ate, drank, and slept was not more than twelve feet square. The ordinary rules of decency, or anything approaching them, cannot exist here, for in such loathsome dens, decency is simply impossible in practice.

"The courts and alleys are worse than the front streets. Entering one, you find yourself in a little narrow passage without pavement, full of holes, filled with dirty water, or the domestic refuse of the houses. The faces you meet are not pleasant to look upon. They are those of women who have led troubled and burdensome lives—lives without the light of domestic affection—of young girls prematurely old, and young men and boys upon whom vice has already too plainly placed its trademark. The odours of the court are abominable, and the causes from which they spring cannot be described here.

"There are drunkards, and brawlers, and wife-beaters by scores. John Barleycorn reigns lord of all the district. In hardly any house on Saturday night can you see the father, sometimes not the mother. The room is crowded with children; there is no appearance of marketing. Where is the wife or mother? She probably wears a black eye as a tribute to the marital affection of her husband, or she is pouring bitter oaths and curses on the devoted heads of the children. Ask for the 'good man,' and the woman laughs at the epithet, and tells you, you will find him at the 'pub.' The place is honeycombed with public-houses, and these are crammed to the doors, and one of the most sickening sights is to see women hunting for their husbands, to obtain the price of Sunday's dinner ere the week's wages are spent in drink. But often it is the toddling child, crying pitifully, who comes to search both for father and mother, who are to be found in a state of semi-drunkenness at the bar.

"Worse still, numbers of young men and women are found in these places, and as midnight tolls the people reel out in the worst state of inebriety. Then the wife-beating, the domestic jangles, the immorality, begins. The young people very often begin life without the formality of marriage, but many of them marry ultimately, and beginning in this undesirable fashion, live as their neighbours live, chiefly in the public-house, and die only to be buried by the parish, or the insurance society, to which, by hook or by crook, even the worst among these miserable people have contrived to pay their penny a week."

I am thankful to add that, as a result of the appeals in the Society's Magazine, at the Mansion House, at public meetings in London and the provinces, and also by "press notices" of the moral condition of the neighbourhood, funds were sent sufficient to enable the Committee to place five additional missionaries in the "moral wastes" before referred to. In addition to this help—for which we praise God—the members of one family left the Society, at different periods, over thirty thousand pounds, being moved to do so under God, by the above appeal.

ANNUAL TEA MEETINGS.

These were great occasions, and the converts of the Mission would try to induce many of their relations and old companions to come. The Tea Meetings were usually held in the Methodist Chapel in "Cooper's Gardens," adjoining my district. Different gentlemen who took an interest in the work, presided, and on two occasions Mr. F. A. Bevan, who is now the Society's Treasurer, filled the chair. On the first occasion, about thirty-three years ago, he had been requested by his honoured father, the late Mr. R. L. C. Bevan, to come and see some of the characters that I had described at a public meeting, over which the latter had presided. He was so pleased with all he saw and heard that he kindly offered to come again. The next visit was at the close of my ten years' work in the district, when he again presided. It was a crowded meeting, and several ministers and missionaries gave soul-stirring addresses. The singing was grand, for some of the old " free and easy " boys, who sat together, gave full breath to the songs of Zion, which made the walls of the old Chapel resound.

The Chairman remarked how their faces shone while they were singing, and he gave them some very encouraging counsel to persevere, exhorting each one to consider himself a messenger from God, and work while it was day.

This brings to a close the fourth decade of my life.

" All hail the power of Jesu's name,
　　Let angels prostrate fall ;
　Bring forth the royal diadem,
　　And crown Him Lord of All.

　Sinners, whose love can ne'er forget
　　The wormwood and the gall ;
　Go, spread your trophies at his feet,
　　And crown Him Lord of All."

FIFTH DECADE.

I WAS still prosecuting my work for God in the district when I entered this period of my life, but before the close of the first year I was called upon to make another change. The Secretary—the Rev. John Garwood—informed me that a friend having given a sum of money to provide an additional missionary to public-houses for twelve years, the Committee had decided to appropriate it to the extensive parish of Shoreditch.

In his usual kind way, he asked me to take up this work, saying they were of opinion that I was adapted for it, adding, "You must look upon it as a kind of promotion." This proposed change came as a shock, and I shrunk from it and began to urge reasons why I should remain where I was, as I felt there were others who were better fitted to take up the new work. Every reason that I put forward against the change he used in favour of it. He asked me to think about it, and pray about it, as there was no need to hurry, and he trusted I should be led to the right conclusion.

On mentioning the subject to my dear wife, who had always been such a great help in the work, she exclaimed, "This is the very work that you always said you could not possibly do, and now the Committee want to appoint you to it." The more I thought of

L

it, the greater the difficulties appeared. I had laboured for years in opening up the district, and by the blessing of God had succeeded in getting a few local friends to form themselves into a committee and had thus secured a permanent Mission Station. Here a work for God had been carried on for several years, as the foregoing chapters will show. The Secretary of the Mission Station, when the Annual Public Meeting was held, read a report, Mr. F. A. Bevan again presiding, from which I make a few extracts.

> "The work of the past year has been carried on with increased energy, the simple object of the missionary and those working with him, has been to bring under the sound of the Gospel the careless, the ignorant, the abandoned, and the depraved. Hundreds of such have been induced to listen to the message of reconciliation, with the result that some have been saved. The meetings have been well sustained, both on Sundays and week-evenings, but the room has become too small, and the Committee pray that God may open a way for securing a larger place so that more good might be done and numbers of men saved from the ruinous effects of public-houses.
>
> "The sixteen loan-tract visitors have made—in addition to the missionary's own visitation—upwards of twenty thousand visits, and exchanged as many tracts. The Committee are very thankful to the Lord of the harvest for these labourers, and we are all prepared to lay ourselves out for greater efforts in the coming year."

Now I must confess that when I thought of the prayers and efforts that had been bestowed in getting this machinery into working order, I felt no little concern about any change that might affect its continuance. The reader can, therefore, understand the cause of my deep anxiety. But,

> "God moves in a mysterious way,
> His wonders to perform."

At times He teaches us truly that we are nothing.

I now informed the local friends and workers of the change which the Parent Committee had decided upon, and I succeeded in getting them to promise to sustain the work as heretofore.

A PRELIMINARY SKIRMISH.

Just at this time the Secretary sent for me again and said that they wished me to go to Colchester for a month's work among the Militia, as the brother who had been sent down to do that work had returned, not being able to carry it on, for the men were billeted in public-houses. I was told that it would be a good preparation for my future work, and such it surely was, for a rougher time in visiting public-houses I scarcely ever had.

I left at once, for the work was waiting, and after an interview with the lady (Miss Francis) who sustained the work among these rough characters, I sallied forth to the conflict, provided with the "Sword of the Spirit," and some small ammunition. It was real sharp hand-to-hand fighting in most of the houses, for some of the men were often the worse for drink, and as one can imagine there was plenty of ridicule, banter, and often gross insult to face.

Besides visiting them in the houses where they were quartered, and getting among them on the parade ground, we started an evening school in the " Soldier's Home " for those who were anxious to learn, some of them being terribly ignorant, as the Education Act was not then in operation. Several tea meetings were also held, at which we succeeded in getting most of the men under the sound of the Gospel.

The honorary Chaplain, who was a Vicar in the town, was asked to preside at the first gathering. He smiled, and said, " I will come, but the men won't stay to hear anything, for after they have had their tea they will go; why, they would not come to Church, only they are compelled."

Over two hundred men came to the first gathering. I told them what had been said, and in order to prove that the idea was wrong, hoped they would stay to the meeting which would last about twenty minutes. The Chaplain presided, and I described the story of David and the giant Goliath. When I reached the point in the narrative where David had his sling and stones, and was hastening to meet the giant—at which point the attention of all seemed rivetted—I stopped, and said our time was gone and we would close. The shouting was deafening as the whole body of men cried out, " Go on, Go on." We did so, and at the close most of the men knelt while prayer was offered, and the Chairman asked that he might come again, as he had never seen anything like it before.

Reading the Scriptures, distributing Christian literature, urging the claims of the Gospel during the daily visitations to the men, visiting the sick, and arranging tea and public meetings, these were the means of inducing many to lead better lives, and some to repentance and faith in Christ.

Much more might be said of the work carried on among this body of men, both at this training time and in subsequent years, but it must suffice to say that at the close of that training the townspeople were greatly surprised to find the men had gone to their homes quietly.

On former occasions, when the Regiment was disbanded, there were often terrible scenes of drunkenness, fighting, and even smashing shop windows in the town, and I was told that the railway station, on one occasion, presented the appearance of a slaughter house, as the militia, in their drunken fury, had driven off the officials, and, maiming those who had charge of a train, took possession of it. A fierce fight began among themselves, for some of the calmer spirits were determined that the infuriated men should not move the train. The military had to be sent from garrison to quell the riot and to protect the railway servants.

A special meeting was convened in the town a few days later, at which I gave an account of the work of the Mission, when the Chairman and others expressed the thanks of many in the town to the lady friend and the London City Mission for the marvellous improvement in the conduct of the militia.

FAREWELL TO THE OLD FIELD.

When I arrived home I was informed that a probationer was about to be appointed to my much-loved district, while a tea and public meeting were arranged by the local friends to bid me farewell. Mr. William Fox, an old friend of the Mission, presided. Over five hundred were present, and several local ministers and friends gave addresses. A report was read by the local secretary, which was far too eulogistic, but I will just give an extract from the local paper.

> "The Chairman said he had known the missionary's work for some years, had marked its growth, and was thankful for what had been accomplished. He was rather sorry that the Committee had decided to remove their friend, but he hoped he would be very useful in his new work, and that his successor, who is with us to-night, might be encouraged in carrying on the work.
>
> "The Rev. Wm. Cuff said he felt regret at the change, for he knew of the work which had been done for several years past. Still, he was convinced that the hand of God was in it. He described the new work as most difficult, as 'bearding the lion in his den,' and if ever a man needed grace and moral courage, he does for that work."

I am thankful to say that the work has been, and is being, successfully carried on by my successor to this day, and that in course of time a new Mission Hall was built.

I may also note here that my dear friend, Ned, was asked about this time to go to Northampton to continue a Mission which had been started in a disused "Circus." He remained in that town for over twenty-five years, accomplishing a blessed work for the Saviour he loved, until he was called Home a few years since.

AT THE OUTPOSTS.

My new district contained the parishes of Shoreditch, Hoxton, and Haggerstone, a large area in which I found over 500 public-houses and coffee shops. This was my field of operation, virgin soil, so to speak, for it had never been visited by a missionary before. I need scarcely say that vice and crime abounded to an awful degree, but I was sent to carry the Gospel to the most abandoned, and I found it in truth to be a case of "bearding the lion in his den."

Opposition in its bitterest form had to be met, and hand to hand conflicts waged continually. It was, indeed, the enemy's ground, and to carry on a Christian campaign in these places or "outposts" was extremely difficult. "What will happen next?" said one man. "Only think, they want to bring religion into our public-houses, but we will soon stop that little game."

I have often been asked, "What can you do with the Gospel in public-houses?" My answer is, "We do the best we can." I will try and show in the following pages the method of working at the "outposts," the variety of material or character there is to war against, the weapons we use, and the results.

THE METHOD OF WORK.

I started out on the first morning to my new work with that prayer continually on my lips, "Lord, help me." The first thing I did on entering was to introduce myself to the landlord, or the man in charge of the bar, before dealing with the customers. I found this plan answered very well during the whole time I was engaged in this work, for if you once get the good-will of the proprietor the whole house is open to you. Some of the proprietors were very suspicious, being under the impression that if my work succeeded, theirs would suffer, so, of course, it was clearly evident I was not wanted, for if I found any nefarious traffic being carried on I should certainly war against it. One land-lord—whom I knew to be carrying on an illegal busi-ness—would not allow me on the premises, telling me in a most abusive manner that if I called again he would throw me into the street. I tried to reason with him, but he would not hear me. I left him, warning him to be careful, or the next time I called he might be missing. On my next visit I found the house was "under new management," the former landlord having been turned out.

THREE TYPICAL STAGES.

The landlord of a public-house, who always received me courteously, asked me one day how I got on with the proprietors of the houses I visited. I answered that the majority were getting to know me, and gave me permission to visit their houses.

"How do you get on with my neighbour over the way?" he asked.

"Fairly well, now," I answered, "though he was most difficult at first."

"I often stand at this window," said he, "and look at those three buildings opposite, for they represent the three stages through which many of the people pass in this neighbourhood."

"What are they?" I enquired.

"Well," said he, "the first one is the Church where most people go at least once in their lives—to get married. The next one is the public-house, and no doubt numbers spend as much time there as possible, and all the money they can get. The third one is the workhouse, where many who can no longer work, and have no more money to spend, are obliged to go, and there spend their last days, to be buried by the parish."

Now, it is about my first visit to this house, which stands between the Church and the workhouse, that I want to say a little. It was one fine night when the house was full of customers that I entered the large space in front of the bar. It was brilliantly lighted, and it was quite apparent that nothing had been spared to make it attractive. I addressed myself to the landlord, and asked him to accept one of my little books, as possibly some one in the family might like to read it. With a torrent of abuse he told me my place was in the street, and the sooner I got there the better it would be for me.

"If I want any religion," said he, "I can get all I want next door for twopence."

The chief barman from the other side then came forward and asked what was the matter. His master told him I wanted to thrust religion down his throat, and he would not have it. Then both of them abused me, and when they had exhausted themselves, I said,

"Gentlemen, I am very sorry if I have said anything to cause you to be angry, for I simply asked would you accept a little good reading? If you don't want it I will take it back, but I don't know why you should get into such a rage."

"Well," they cried out, "we neither want you nor your religion, so get outside."

As I was leaving the house the men in the bar, perhaps out of pity, for they had heard the volume of abuse I had received, asked me for something to read. I gave several papers which contained extracts from Lord Shaftesbury's speech in the House of Lords, on the Vivisection Bill. One man, as soon as he looked at it, said, "Why, landlord, here is the very thing we have been talking about, Lord Shaftesbury's speech in the House of Lords." The landlord gave a little grunt, and I left an extra copy, should he like to read it.

In course of time I came round to this house again. It was night, and a strange sensation came over me as I thought of "bearding the lion in his den," but having made up my mind when undertaking this work that I would not pass by any house, if possible, I had to enter. One peculiar feature is that there is no knocking at doors. No, the doors of public-houses swing open very easily, and you can never tell what awaits you when inside. Sometimes you may have to leave the place sooner than you wish, or you are detained longer than is desirable.

I entered and found that the bar where I had such a bad reception last time was full of people and the landlord was in charge. I thought it wiser to do a little work among the people on the further side of the house before confronting the landlord, and so I opened the door on which the following words were written in gilt letters, " Glasses only," which meant that the better class customer entered that way. I passed along and found about half a dozen gentlemen engaged in conversation over their glasses. After apologizing for intruding, I asked them to accept a little good reading. They each took one, and began perusing the contents, after which one said,

" Why, this is about religion, are you a clergyman? "

"No," I replied, "I am a missionary to public-houses."

"A missionary to public-houses!" said another. "I never heard of such a mission before; there are several mission-boxes in my home, and I'll take this little book home to my wife, and tell her it was given to me by a missionary to public-houses." "You must not think," said another, "that because we are here we are regular drinkers. No, we are here to transact a little business."

"I don't altogether neglect these things," said one, "for I go to a place of worship sometimes."

"Gentlemen," I replied, "I suppose you were all more or less taught about these good things in your younger days, and I want to remind you of the good old Book that God has given to be our guide through life, and of the Saviour it makes known to us, Who alone is able to save us from sin and its terrible consequences."

They all said they should not forget what they had just heard, and one asked, "How do you get on with the landlords?" "As a rule I get on very well when we come to know each other," I replied.

I saw the landlord near by while we were thus chatting, and on my way out I asked him if he would accept one of my books.

"Well, just a minute," said he, "don't you parsons say that we publicans are all sinners?"

"Certainly," I replied.

"Then," with a curl of the lip, he said, "I should like to know what you are?"

"Well, Sir, I'm a sinner, too."

"Now, that caps all that ever I heard. Do you mean to say that *all* are sinners, for I want to understand you correctly?"

"I don't want you to take my word for it," said I, "this is the Word of God, the Bible, which perhaps you were accustomed to read in your young days," and so referring him to the third Chapter of Romans, I quoted, "'There is none righteous, no, not one. . . . . . For all have sinned and come short of the glory of God.' . . . . 'All we like sheep have gone astray; we have turned every one to his own way, and the Lord hath laid on Him (Jesus Christ) the iniquity of us all' (Isaiah liii. 6)." I added, "If there is any difference between you and me, it is simply this, that I, a poor, lost and hell-deserving sinner have trusted in the Lord Jesus Christ for Salvation, and I want you to do the same."

"Yes," said he, "I'll have one of your books, and I'll read it, too, and I am sure my wife will, for she reads her prayer-book every Sunday afternoon."

I was always a welcome visitor in the house after that, and I had some very good times there. I do not know how far the efforts put forth in this house led the proprietor and his wife to a better life, but I do know that their only child became deeply interested in good things through reading our literature, and through conversations held across the bar. The boy had a missionary box for some years in which he collected good sums, and his father told me that both he and his mother had ultimately decided to let the boy have his own way, and go to college to be trained for a missionary instead of following their own mode of life. After leaving the district I heard that he was getting on well, and his parents had left the " line."

At another house in a busy thoroughfare, where a good brisk business was carried on, the wife was a member of a Church near by, and she had a weekly meeting for the poor in a room on the premises. The house was closed on Sundays, and no person was served who was the worse for drink. There were two daughters, who were just growing into womanhood, and I was often asked into the bar-parlour to read and talk with them. I had many good opportunities of setting forth the Gospel among the customers, and perhaps I felt more freedom from realizing that I had the sympathy of the proprietor and his wife.

Some time afterwards the landlord asked me into the parlour, as they wanted to consult me on an important question. The man, in the presence of his wife and family, said, with deep emotion,

" We have been considering for some time whether we should get out of this line or not, and we thought we should like to know what you think about the question."

" It is a difficult matter to advise you upon," I replied, " for if I answer from my own standpoint, and the work I am trying to do, I should say, stay. The house is well conducted, I have never seen an intoxicated person in it, and it is closed all day on Sundays. If, however, I answer from your standpoint, and that of your daughters, I should say, leave it, but I pray God to lead you to the right decision."

We had a little prayer about the matter and they decided to leave the place. They took a " Temperance Hotel," where some members of the family are carrying it on to this day, while the house they left passed into the hands of people who opened it on Sundays, and it soon went down to the level of many others in the neighbourhood.

Such was my method of work in public-houses and coffee-shops that I visited.

I will now pass on to notice the variety of characters I met with, the weapons used, and the results.

Some of the houses in the main roads leading to the City would be mostly frequented by fairly well-to-do people, while those in slum neighbourhoods would be used by the " riff-raff " of society. It will at once be seen that the way of dealing with one class must be very different from the manner of meeting the other, but the main weapon used in this battle-field is the same as in the former field, namely, the Bible. Let me instance what I mean.

THE BIBLE VICTORIOUS.

In one of the "private compartments" in a large house of a leading thoroughfare, I found some gentlemen who were evidently ready for a contest. I was soon confronted with a series of questions, which I answered, as far as possible, from the Bible. My antagonist, now waxing warm, began to denounce the Bible and its teachings, and as for religious folk and those who believed that Book he would not trust them as far as he could see them. After he had railed at the Bible and all those who believed in it, I asked him to pause and allow me to speak. To this they all agreed.

"Now, gentlemen," said I, "perhaps every one of you believe that this Book contains truths and precepts which are right, and to a great extent you conform to them."

Their spokesman vehemently protested when I said, "Will you allow me to try and prove it?" This being agreed to, I continued,

"May I ask if any of you are employers of labour?"

"Yes, he employs a number of men," said one, pointing to their spokesman.

"Well, Sir," I asked, "when you want a man to fill a responsible post, as cashier or keeper of valuable stores, how do you secure one?"

"I mostly advertise," he answered.

"Yes," I replied, "and do you put in the advertisement that the man must be a liar, a drunkard, a thief, and an idler, or do you say that he must be truthful, sober, honest, and industrious?"

"You certainly do not think that I am daft, do you?" said he. "Who would be such a fool as to advertise in that way. We want the best men we can get for those positions, and advertise accordingly, but what has that to do with the question?"

"Just this," I replied. "You admit that the man who believes and seeks to live according to the teaching of this Book secures your best positions, and you will not trust them to men who openly and constantly violate the same."

They all admitted the conclusion and several of them said they had been brought up to believe the Bible, and they knew it was a good Book, while the chief speaker said :—

"I frankly admit my mother was a great believer in the Bible, and if ever there was a good woman, she was one."

I gave them a little suitable reading and exhorted them to read the Scriptures, for they contained the Words of Eternal Life. They thanked me for what I had said, and promised they would think about it.

A COMPANY OF THIEVES.

There is a certain house down a side street which usually had some very strange customers. There never seemed to be any persons at the bar, and yet I was

M

sure I could hear voices not far away. Hearing these one day, while in conversation with the landlord, I asked permission to visit them, but he said, "You cannot go in there except you belong to their community." After arguing the point, he said, "As I know you only want to do them good go in and try your luck." So saying, he opened a bar-counter door, and I passed through to a little inner-room, out of which a door opened into the room whence I had heard the sound of voices.

After warning me as to what I might have to face he opened the door and introduced me as a friend of his, who wanted to have a talk with them. The place was fairly well filled, and as soon as the men saw me some made a dash to open the window and spring out, but the landlord called out, "It's all right, keep quiet." (I may mention that in some houses when entering certain rooms it was no uncommon thing to see those who did not know me spring through the window, for I suppose they still imagined I was a detective.) The landlord retired, closing the door after him, and I was shut in with a company of thieves!

Some of them began to ask me questions, others explained how they were out of work, being jewellers from Birmingham. I told them I wanted their attention for a few minutes while I read or sang, or preached to them.

The majority wanted a sermon. "Then," said I,

"we must have a text." I opened my Bible at the thirty-second chapter of Numbers, and read from the 23rd verse these words :—"Be sure your sin will find you out." I described what sin was—according to the Scriptures—and how it would find us all out; how it had found some out whom I had known, who were now in penal servitude, how it had found out others whom it had led to the place of public execution. "Perhaps," I added, "it may have found out some one here present who has suffered for it, but whatever it may be sin will, at the Great Assize, find us all out." I then related how my sin had found me out some years ago, and being deeply convicted by the Word of God, and my own conscience, I cried to God for mercy, and trusting Christ and His atoning work on the Cross for poor sinners, I obtained full Salvation from the guilt and power of sin. I assured them that the same blessings could be theirs if they repented of their sins, and turned to God with full purpose of heart.

Some listened very quietly, while a good deal of whispering was going on with another little gang. One asked, "Were you once the Chaplain of Pentonville?" I said, "No." "Then you preached sometimes to the prisoners there, didn't you?" Again I answered, "No." Turning to one of his mates, he continued, "Didn't we hear this gentleman preach there the Sunday before we came out?" "Yes," he answered, and turning to me he said, "I knew you again the moment you entered this room, and you know that was the very text and sermon you preached on that Sunday." I told them I was glad they remembered the text and the sermon, and hoped they would all think seriously of what I had said to them. While I was giving some suitable reading to those who could read and who would receive it, I overheard one man say to another, "Arn't you coming out, it's after four o'clock?" "No," said he, "I'm not going out to-day." "No more shall I," said another, "it's took all the steam out of me for to-day, this has."

After thanking them for their attention, and the landlord for allowing me the opportunity of speaking, I left, but had not gone far away before a young man overtook me, and after thanking me for my warning and advice, he said, "I have an excellent watch here that I will sell you at a bargain if you will buy it." I told him I had a watch, and urged him to give up his mode of life and seek to obtain an honest living. He looked at me and said, "I only wish I *could* do as you advise, but I can't," and he ran away.

AMONG "CARD SHARPERS."

I was not always so well received by the thieving and gambling fraternity as on the occasion last noticed. I have often been threatened with violence, but I only remember one instance when it actually took place. I entered a house one Monday morning, in a room of which was a company of well-dressed men.

IN OTHER WARS.

Some were changing money at the bar, and I discovered that they were "card sharpers," or "swell-mobsmen," who, having been successful on the Sunday in fleecing poor dupes, were now engaged in exchanging their heavily-weighted pockets of copper and silver for gold or notes.

The house had a bad reputation in the neighbourhood. The landlord, no doubt, got a good monetary return for allowing this class of gentry to use the place, but it was not long before the licence was withheld, and the house was ultimately demolished.

I had met some of these men before, and was busy conversing with a small group when up came a strange man from behind and gave me a severe slap on the side of my head, which almost dazed me for a moment. Taking off my hat and rubbing my head, I asked, "Has that hurt your hand, Sir?" for I felt sure he wanted to intimidate me by his action, and I resolved, by God's help, to be victor. He defiantly said, "What do you mean?" I calmly replied, "I suppose you thought my head was soft, but you have found it is not." The others all gathered round, and the door was closed, not knowing what might happen. Of course this was no place to show the white feather, so addressing my assailant, I said,

"I want to tell you, in the presence of these gentlemen, that you have made a mistake in your action this morning. I may say, in the first place, that, but for the grace of God, you might not be standing there now, and in the second place that this is probably not the last time I shall meet you, for you have laid yourself open to grave consequences."

" What is your profession, then? " he asked.

" I am a Christian public-man," I replied, " and my work is to try and make this world better. I know what your profession is, very well, and probably we shall meet again."

A hurried consultation took place among some of them, and then laying hold of my assailant, one said, " You had no right to interfere with this man. He comes here to try and do us good, and if you do not at once make a full and frank apology to him we shall give you a thrashing." The man made an apology, which I accepted, and, giving them a little further counsel, I left the house.

I felt the effects of that visit, both mentally and physically, for days and nights afterwards.

These spiritual and mental conflicts in which I had to be so often engaged had to be fought over again in my quiet moments as I tried to discover any point in which I had been the loser, and then I did not sleep until I had thought out the most effectual manner of dealing with the same. In this way I was able, by reading and prayer, to place almost every possible argument concerning the existence of God, the Bible, our Lord Jesus Christ, Christian characters, etc., under one or other of about half a dozen headings, or classes, so that when an opponent started his objection I knew.

at once in which class to place him, and how to deal with him.

One can easily imagine that a work of this kind is a severe strain upon the worker and that it takes a great deal out of him to be constantly battling with sin and sinners in public-houses. This is, indeed, the enemy's ground, and aggressive work truly means "bearding the lion in his den." Yet in every company of men or women, however abandoned, I could always find those to whom I could appeal for fair play or reason. There were always some in every bar who were eager for the fray, and they would commence asking all kinds of questions, some reasonable and others very foolish. I tried to answer their questions, as far as possible, from the Bible, because it brought the Word of God to bear on them, and also because if they rejected the answer given therein I could enforce upon them the fact that that was the highest, in fact, the final court of appeal. I always found the Word of God victorious, and stood firm to its teachings, however bitter and hostile the opposition. I will here give one or two illustrations.

MATERIALISM AND THE BIBLE.

I found a large company of men drinking in a certain public-house one night, and some of them were "three sheets in the wind," a saying which indicates that they were in a lively go-ahead mood. I had not been talking long before a man came and asked what Book I had in my hand. I said, "The Bible."

"Well, I don't believe in it," said he.

One of the rules I had laid down for my guidance with questioners and cavillers was never to remain on the defensive longer than possible, but to put my opponent on the defensive, so I answered,

"I never said you did, but may I ask what you do believe in?"

"Why, I'm a materialist, and believe in nature and natural laws."

"Then may I ask what is nature?"

"Why, everything is nature, this floor is nature," and here he took his pipe out of his mouth and emphasized his declaration by stamping his foot on the floor.

"And what are natural laws?" said I.

"Natural laws are the laws of nature," he replied.

"Now will you tell me what is the first law of nature?"

"Nobody can argue a scientific question in this way, but if you like to discuss any branch of science with me, astronomy, or geology, or any other, one of these gentlemen will be chairman, and I'm your man."

"I'm afraid I do not know much about science," I replied, "but if there is anything good in your creed I shall be glad to know it, and so I thought we might start at the beginning. You are a materialist and believe in nature and natural laws. You say that everything is nature, and natural laws are the laws of nature. Now, I simply want to know which is the first law of nature?''

''I tell you,'' he answered, with warmth, ''that no scientist argues like that.''

''I don't know how scientists argue,'' I replied, ''but I know how I would answer a plain question about what I believed in. If you asked me what was the first command of God in this Bible I would tell you, but you say you don't believe in God, or the Bible, but in materialism, and I want you to tell me what is the first law in your creed.''

''You don't understand the subject,'' he replied.

''Now, gentlemen,'' I said, addressing the company, ''I was in a public-house a short time ago, and offering a gentleman one of my little books, he said, 'No, thank you, I don't believe in spiritual or eternal things. I'm a materialist, and believe in nature and nature's laws.' I asked him, 'What is the first law of nature?' and he at once replied, 'The first law of nature is self-preservation, or taking care of yourself.' ''

Our friend, stepping to the front again, said, '' Yes, gentlemen, that is quite right. Every materialist knows that. The first law is to take care of number one, and that is the most important law. He was quite right.''

Up to this time he had been scanning me very closely, so taking two steps backward I looked at him from top to toe, which caused all eyes to be fixed on him. He was wretchedly clad, and nearly bare-foot, so I quietly asked, "My friend, do you keep that law?" For a moment there was a pause, then one of the men said, "Tom, put that in your pipe and smoke it, that's enough for you to think of for some time to come."

Our friend was not to be so easily subdued, so rushing up to me, he seized my coat and exclaimed, "You are like all parsons, you know how to look after number one. You have better clothes on now than I can get on Sundays, and I'll guarantee you had a better dinner to-day than I had on Sunday." Then turning to those present he asked, "Doesn't he look as though he took good care of himself?" To this they all assented.

"Then I am the best materialist, Tom," I said.

"How do you make that out?" said he.

"You admit," I replied, "that the first law in your creed is self-preservation, or looking after number one, and you have just told all present that I keep that law better than you do, therefore I *must* be the best materialist."

Those present begged Tom to stop, as he had got plenty to think about if he would give his mind to it, while they all admitted the argument was properly closed. I asked permission for a little more of their time in order to tell them how I became such a good materialist. To this they willingly assented.

I opened my Bible and said, "This Book you say

you do not believe in. Listen while I read what it says on this question, 'Seek ye first the Kingdom of God, and His righteousness, and all these things (food and raiment) shall be added unto you' (Matt. vi. 33). 'For Godliness is profitable unto all things, having promise of the life that now is, and of that which is to come' (1st Tim. iv. 8). This Book has taught me to trust in Christ as my Saviour and King. It has taught me to care for myself and those belonging to me. It has taught me to care for others, and try to bring them into this blessed life, and that is why I am here to-night. Now, gentlemen, and especially you, Tom, I commend this Book to you as being able to make you wise unto Salvation, so that your lives may be true and useful here, and your future life one of bliss and happiness."

I shortly afterwards left the house, and hearing a voice behind calling me, I looked round and saw Tom.

"You must excuse me," he said, "but I should like another word with you. I never heard that argument put in that way before, and I feel all to pieces."

"My friend," said I, "have you not read your Bible in days gone by?"

"Yes, Sir, I have one at home, but I've neglected it since associating with free-thinkers and men who drink, but I mean to stop that kind of life. I am going home to read the Old Book, and by God's help I'll lead a new life."

CONCENTRATED FIRING.

It used to be the practice in former days—I don't know if it is so now—when an army was besieging a strongly fortified position, to bombard the place by artillery, and their chief object was to try and make a breach at some point for the storming party to enter. To accomplish this the different batteries would concentrate their firing on one point until a breach was made.

The work of our Mission may be said to be a kind of concentrated firing in its efforts to bombard and take the "City of Mansoul." Its agents have the Holy Bible placed in their hands, and they are instructed to go among the people in their districts and teach what it says about man as a sinner, and the Redemption wrought out for men by Jesus Christ.

I will illustrate what I mean by the following :—

One Sunday evening while devout worshippers were in the various houses of prayer I sallied forth to try and do a little work for the Master in bars and tap-rooms. As I entered the first bar of a house and was speaking to the landlord I noticed a man take up his pot of beer and leave the place. I asked the landlord why he had left in such a hurry, and he said, " I think you must have frightened him; if, however, you go round to the end bar you will find him there." I went round to that compartment and at once addressed the man, saying, " Did I frighten you that you ran out of the other bar, or did your conscience tell you it was Sunday night, and you ought not to be there?"

"Well, perhaps it was a little of both, but how is it," he asked, "that you are after me so much, at least, you and others like you?"

"I do not understand what you mean."

"Well," he said, "when I'm at work in the shop a man comes in and gives me something to read, and tells me I'm a sinner and that Christ wants to save me, and that unless I repent I must perish. When I walk along the street some one else gives me some reading and tells me the same kind of tale. When I go home my wife shows me something left for me to read and says a man called and invited us to some meeting, as we ought to seek to get right with God. This morning I went down to the River Lea, or as it is called, the working man's Brighton, in order to get a little fresh air and enjoy a bit of fun, and there I saw you preaching along with a number of others, and as I listened I heard the same things stated and I had to go away. At dinner I told my wife about it and said, 'It does not matter where I go, I'm sure to meet some of these men, but I'll go for a little while this evening where they won't find me. I'll go to the public-house.' And now, blow me, if you don't come in here. I don't think I am worse than other men that you should always be on my track hunting me about."

I calmly reasoned with him and assured him that it was not simply man who was after him, but that it was God, Who earnestly desired his Salvation, that he might be happy in His love and service here, and throughout eternity. I found that he had been the subject of many prayers, and that both he and his wife had been trained to read their Bible. I urged upon him the claims of Christ and besought him to cease the strife against God, and yield to the striving of the Holy Spirit.

Looking at me earnestly, he said,

"I believe it must be as you say, for this has been going on for some time and it must be ended. I thank you for your words; I'll go home, and by God's help, we'll start a new life."

WOMEN DRAM DRINKERS.

It is a painful sight to see a man abandoned to dram drinking, but it is infinitely worse to see a woman wholly given up to the vice. Alas, there are many such.

I met a woman who used to glory in making younger ones drunkards, and she would stand at the street corners, near public-houses, to allure them to their destruction. She laughingly said to me, "I'll make more women drunk than you can make sober." She succeeded to a great extent in her hellish designs.

This habit of "dram drinking" was practised by many women from the cradle, and even to the grave. Weddings, births, christenings, birthdays, and funerals were great events for drinking parties when friends gathered at a public-house, if there were not sufficient room in their little home.

One day I found a number of women in mourning garb, in a public-house, drinking together. One woman was weeping bitterly, apparently sorely grief-stricken, while a little girl was clinging to her dress, also crying bitterly. I tried to comfort them from God's Holy Word when one of the women, beckoning to me, quietly said,

" She is my sister, and she is crying because she has just buried two of her children who died with fever. I wish I could get her home, for she has been drinking terribly."

I spoke words of sympathy to the poor heart-broken mother, and told her of God Who could heal her spirit. She listened while I besought her to go home and drink no more. All at once she fixed her gaze on me and cried out,

" Don't talk to me of God! Why did He take my children from me? I loved my children, but now I love nothing but this," and taking up a glass of rum from the counter, she said,

" I'll drink it while I live, I'll drink it when I'm dying, and then I know I shall go to hell and be d——d ! "

So saying she drank the contents before anyone could get it from her, and reeling into the corner fell with a scream. Her friends got her home and I went on my way feeling very sad at heart, that it was possible for a woman to love nothing so much as " dram drinking."

A SURPRISE CORNER.

Visiting a house that was mostly well patronized, especially by women, I was confronted by an elderly woman who held in her hand a glass of rum. Turning to the other women, she said,

" As soon as this gentleman came in at the door I thought, now here comes one who will have a glass of rum with me; you will, won't you, Sir? "

I held up my hand to silence her, but she persistently continued,

" I'm sure you will have this with me, for I know you have a great respect for women, I can tell by the colour of your eye ! "

A very hearty continuous laugh was raised by the company of women present at what they thought was a " good fall " taken out of the missionary by their champion, who still stood before me with the glass in her hand.

As soon as they became a little quiet, I again raised my hand, and addressing the woman said,

" You have spoken the truth; I have a great respect for women, and I want to tell you why. The first reason why I respect women is, because my mother was a woman." At this they all laughed, and I continued, " The second reason why I respect women is because the first person who took my hands, and placing them together, while bending at her knee, taught my lips to lisp that beautiful prayer, beginning, Our Father, Which art in Heaven,' was a woman, my mother, and although she died when I was a boy, leaving me to struggle alone in the world, she taught me of Jesus and the way to Heaven. After a roaming life, during which I suffered many hardships, I returned to the village where I was born and visited the churchyard where my mother and some of my ancestors lay buried, and taking off my hat I raised my eyes to heaven and thanked God that I had had a good mother. Now let me beseech you mothers so to teach your children about Jesus and the way to Heaven, that when you are laid in the grave they may sometimes visit the spot and drop a tear, and thank God for having had a good mother."

Before I had finished speaking I noticed that the woman had put down the glass of rum, and most of them were wiping their eyes with their aprons. The woman who had first spoken to me grasped my hand, and with tears in her eyes, exclaimed,

" God bless you, Sir; go and tell that to all the mothers in Shoreditch, for they need it."

FOLLOWING UP CASES.

Among the tens of thousands to whom I have spoken the Word of Life, in public-houses and coffee and dining-rooms, numbers have requested me to call and see them at their homes. Sometimes a word about their early days, or something I may have said, has awakened their memory, and they have at once left the house and taken me to their homes, where personal dealing has resulted in much good being done, not only to the individual himself, but to others around. I will here give a typical case among many others that have occurred.

IN A CLUB HOUSE.

One very cold day while walking along one of the main streets I entered a public-house, and found my way to a large room, full of men. The fire was burning brightly in the grate, and this was a "trade society's club house," and most of the members present were either sick or out of work. They seemed pleased to see me, and before long some of the leading infidels were contesting with me the principles of Christianity.

Near the fire sat a young man, leaning his head on his hand, who evidently found a difficulty in breathing. Laying my hand gently on his shoulder I said,

"My friend, I am afraid you are ill."

"I am, Sir," said the poor man. "I've been to the hospital near here, but being so very cold I came in here for a warm, as this is my club house."

His poor wan face and hard breathing moved me to pity, and to try to help him.

"Now, my friend," said I, "my religion teaches me to care for the bodies of men as well as their souls. Would you like to go into a hospital?"

" Yes, Sir," he answered, " I should like to go into Victoria Park Hospital, but I can't get in."

I told him I would try and get him a letter. He gave me his address, and at his request I promised to call and see him.

" Before I go I should like one more word with you," I said. " Now, while you are seeking the aid of earthly physicians to try and restore your bodily health, let me beseech you to look to the Great Physician—the Lord Jesus Christ—for the Salvation of your soul, so that whether living or dying it may be well with you."

I secured a letter and took it to his lodgings, where I spent some time with him. " I am glad you have come," he said, " for some of my shopmates who were in our club-house that day have been to see me, and said that you were like all the parsons, and you wouldn't try to help an outsider like me."

He told me a little of his history. He was 33 years of age, had been born and brought up in Scotland by well-to-do parents, had been trained in Christian principles, and received a good education. His father built a place of worship and largely supported the ministry.

" I suppose," said the poor man, " I am what you call a ' scape-grace,' for as soon as I had ended my apprenticeship at the engineering trade I went to sea on a large steamer, and I have been wild and abused my constitution, and now I fear consumption has got fast hold of me. I hope if I get in the hospital I shall soon recover a little, and then I must be more careful."

I asked him if his parents, or any of his relations, were living, and he replied, "My parents are dead, and my only sister is the wife of the Rev. ——, a popular minister, not far from here." I asked him if I should call and see them, but at this suggestion he appeared very agitated and wished me not to do so. I again besought him to look to Christ.

He seemed to improve a little while at first in the hospital, but it was only a temporary improvement, for he was soon thrown back by several bad attacks. I continued to visit him, as did also a brother missionary who was the appointed visitor to the hospital. I obtained another letter for him, as the doctors were anxious that he should continue with their treatment. But he grew gradually weaker. At my request he at last consented to see his sister. When she saw her brother she was deeply moved, and I left them alone for a time for I felt the occasion too sacred for a stranger's presence. After a time she called me and thanked me for my kind attention to her poor brother, who, she said, had been a wayward lad, but evidently he had truly repented, and was now wholly trusting in Christ.

I saw him the day before he died. Asking him how he was, he said,

"It is nearly all over, now; I have suffered much, but I shall soon be Home. I thank you for all your kindness. It is all I can do, but God will bless you. I often think how remarkable it was that you should have visited our club-house on that bitterly cold day and met with me. I was a perfect stranger to you, but you at once offered to do all you could for me, and you have been my best earthly friend."

I afterwards saw numbers of his old companions, and could see that his end had caused some of them to think seriously. One day while talking to a publican at the bar a man came in, and seeing me there, said,

"You must excuse me, Sir, but I must speak to you, and ask you for a book."

"I suppose you know me," I said.

"Oh, yes," he replied, "I was a shopmate of poor Jim White's, and was in the club-house when you first met him. I and some of his mates visited him several times before he died, and there is no question that the change they saw in Jim, and his death, has terribly shaken a lot of them. Why, Sir, they were all rank infidels in the club-house that day, and nothing pleased them better than an opportunity to rail against God and religion. They were in their glory when they saw you come in and take out your Bible. They said afterwards your reasoning was good; but what you said to poor Jim at the time, and your kindness to him until he died, knocked the infidelity out of them more than all your arguments. I can tell you that there is not so much said against God and religion by the men now as there used to be."

"LEFT THE LINE."

A good many families "left the line," as they had become impressed by the Truth, and were anxious to lead different lives. I frequently heard of the usefulness of some who had yielded themselves to God.

One who had considerable means went to live in the suburbs, where he helped to build several places of worship, and sought in many ways to be useful.

Another went to live in the place where he was born and had a Mission Hall built, and sought to win souls for Christ.

Others started in different businesses, because they felt they could better serve their God and attend the means of grace with their families.

APPOINTED DISTRICT SECRETARY.

I had had some experience in addressing meetings on behalf of the London City Mission, and early in 1883, after my return from a deputation tour in Scotland, I received from the Rev. T. S. Hutchinson, who had become one of the Secretaries of the Society, a letter telling me of my appointment to the District Secretaryship in the East of London, soon to be vacated by Mr. Parker, who had resigned his post.

After prayerfully considering this offer I was led by God to accept it, and entered upon my new duties at once, not without some anxiety, but Mr. Parker remained with me for one month.

My principal duties were to convene meetings in

public buildings and drawing-rooms for the purpose of making known the work of the Mission and raising funds for its support, to form local committees and associations wherever possible, for the purpose of promoting the interests of the Mission and furthering its objects by placing more missionaries in needy districts.

I may say that in addition to the "East London Auxiliary" I had the working of the "North London Auxiliary," and also "North-West London" assigned to me. I was most heartily welcomed by the Auxiliary Committees and local Associations, and also received help and encouragement from the Secretaries, the Rev. T. S. Hutchinson, M.A., and the Rev. R. Dawson, B.A., and also from my (late) colleagues, Messrs. C. M. Sawell, J. M. Weylland, and H. Pearson.

Most of my friends, as well as those who had been conversant with my work heretofore, thought this new departure was the right one, but there was one exception, and that was my dear wife. She had been accustomed to the soul-winning work of our Christian life, and she said, " I cannot see how you can win souls for Christ in going about to get money." I must confess that her argument made me feel uneasy for a time, until I called to mind a saying of Mr. D. L. Moody's, viz., " I would sooner put ten men to work than do ten men's work."

In addition to attending the existing Committees in the Auxiliaries, I spent my time for the first year or two in trying to get new friends in the extended circle allotted to me.   In each Auxiliary Association both ladies' and gentlemen's committees were formed, and more missionaries were placed in needy districts through their efforts.   Drawing-room and garden meetings were held, and liberal contributions were given in support of the work of God among the poor, and I was much encouraged in the work assigned to me.

On the 16th of May, 1884, was ushered in the Society's Jubilee, and a busy day it was from early morn till late at night.   A breakfast meeting was held at Cannon Street Hotel; in the afternoon a solemn service was held in St. Bartholomew's Church, Gray's Inn Road, when, after a sermon preached by the Rev. E. Hopkins, over five hundred missionaries and friends partook of the Sacrament of the Lord's Supper; then the missionaries and officers went to the Holborn Town Hall, where a tea was provided, and finally they repaired to Exeter Hall, where overflowing, enthusiastic and jubilant public meetings were held.   The large hall was packed to its fullest extent, while more than a thousand people attended the overflow meeting in the lower hall.

The late Seventh Earl of Shaftesbury presided over the meeting in the large hall, and I had the great honour and happy privilege of addressing that enthusiastic gathering on my work in the Mission.

A solemn thought comes to my mind as I pen these

lines, and it is this, that every speaker—including the noble Chairman—on that memorable occasion has passed away, except myself, while only a few remain of those who filled the platform. The question I ask myself is, "Why am I spared?" I know not; God knows. It may be He has something further for me to do or to suffer for His glory. If my feet cannot run so swiftly on His errands of love and mercy as they were wont to do; if I cannot any longer stand in the ranks of the Advance Guard at the outposts, I may perhaps be permitted to render some service still in the Citadel, anyhow I can never cease to love and pray for the dear old Mission, my own "Alma Mater."

The result of the efforts put forth by appeals was such that the Committee were enabled to place more missionaries in the field, and a good sum of money was laid aside as a reserve fund. The Parent Committee published a "Jubilee Volume" entitled, "These Fifty Years," being a complete history of the Society down to that time. It was written by my colleague, Mr. J. M. Weylland, than whom the Mission never possessed a more able or a more graphic writer on the Society's work. His "Round the Tower," "The Man with the Book," etc., as well as the Jubilee volume, may still be obtained at the Mission House. The whole of the Jubilee Year was one of much joy and active loving service.

IN DARK SHADOWS.

But I closed this decade of my life in the shadow of a dark cloud—albeit there was a " silver lining " to it—for my dear wife and partner of my trials and triumphs for about thirty years was called to pass into the presence of her Saviour, Whom she loved so ardently and served so cheerfully. It is not for me to write a high eulogium of her worth and deeds, for her record is on High, but this much I must say, she was a most devoted wife, an affectionate mother (she bore eight children, two of whom died in childhood, while five sons and one daughter were left to mourn their loss), sincere and true friend, especially to the poor, the afflicted, and those in want, and a real help-meet to me in my Mission career. She lived exactly three years after her first attack. Calling her children around her, feeling her end was near, she invoked God's blessing upon them one by one, and asked them to meet her in Heaven. A short time before she departed she gave careful and loving instructions to our only daughter—who was then a young woman capable of managing my affairs—to look after me, and to do all she could to make the home-life happy, so that I might be free from any anxiety at home and be all the more able to prosecute God's work with energy. I am glad to put on record that my daughter has done this faithfully, and that she is still with me to comfort me, and attend to my wants. She has (in addition) looked after different branches of my grand-children left motherless, and some of them are living with us at this time. The last words my dear wife said to me, as she beckoned me to her side, while a seraphic smile lighted up her face, were, "I'm going Home now, I feel so tired and want to rest. You and the children will all come by and bye, for my prayers will not be in vain." She closed her eyes and sweetly fell asleep. Thus passed away one who was far more to me than tongue or pen can express, and whom the whole of her family will never cease to love and remember.

"Sleep on, beloved, sleep and take thy rest,
Lay down thy head upon thy Saviour's breast,
We love thee well, but Jesus loves thee best,
Good-night !

"Only 'Good-night,' beloved—not 'farewell,'
A little while, and all His saints shall dwell
In hallowed union, indivisible—
Good-night !

"Until we meet again before His throne,
Clothed in the spotless robe He gives His own,
Until we know even as we are known,
Good-night ! "

SIXTH DECADE.

FOR some time after we had laid our loved one to rest my life appeared almost a blank. Some advised me to go away for rest and change, but I kept to my post, and found comfort in sorrow, for our Gracious God stood by me and sustained me.

By the help of God I was able to secure a number of drawing-room meetings in the autumn and winter months, and lawn meetings at suburban residences in the summer. I met with much encouragement from a large number of kind friends, many of whom have been called home, but a few are still with us. I will here refer to some of them, and the generous help they rendered to this God-honoured Mission.

MR. AND MRS. JOSEPH GURNEY BARCLAY.

"Knotts Green," Leyton (now partly built over), was the home of Mr. J. G. Barclay and his beloved family. It was a noted centre for holding various religious and philanthropic meetings to plead the cause of God and the poor. The first time I suggested having a garden meeting in their beautiful grounds they graciously consented, and a most successful one it was. We had some excellent addresses, one being by the late Rev. P. B. Power, whose speech was full of pathos

MRS. J. GURNEY BARCLAY.

MR. J. GURNEY BARCLAY.

and force. Mr. Barclay's family and friends, composing the house party, were delighted with it, and our host promised to help me at any time, in any way he could. To the end of their lives, their home, whether at Knotts Green, Brighton, or Cromer, was always accessible to me whenever I wanted to consult them about the Society's work, or ask support for the same. Their hearty cheer and kind hospitality can never be forgotten, and their loving tender hearts were ever ready to sympathize and help the poor and the needy.

On one occasion, after a very large and successful meeting in the grounds, Mr. Barclay asked me to go and speak to four sisters, who were "orphans." They questioned me about the work, and what amount of money it would require to place a missionary in a needy district in East London. I told them that the Committee would place an Agent there on a £50 guarantee being given annually towards his support and the Parent Society would supply the other £50. One of them said, "It seems to me that if we give £50 a year we shall own only half a man, but if we give £100 a year we shall have a whole missionary." They appealed to me, and I told them that the Committee would be glad for them to have a whole missionary, and so they at once gave me a cheque.

Mr. and Mrs. Barclay entertained the whole body of missionaries and officers on the occasion of their annual day in the country at Knotts Green on five different occasions. The last time was on July 17th, 1897. Our kind friends met the large company on the lawn and gave them a hearty welcome. Dinner and tea were provided for the 430 missionaries in a large marquee. After tea a short service was held in the tent, when several encouraging addresses were delivered. A most interesting event then took place. Sir George Williams, who was one of the guests, presented Mr. and Mrs. J. G. Barclay, in the name of the Committee, officers and missionaries, with a beautifully illuminated and framed address, signed by every member of the Committee, by the officers and by twelve missionaries, as representatives of the whole body.

Mr. and Mrs. Barclay—with deep feeling—thanked the donors heartily, and assured them of the great pleasure with which they accepted the gift.

This was the last public function that Mr. Barclay attended. He passed away on April 25th, 1898, in his 82nd year. He was the oldest member of the Mission and one of its most liberal supporters. He joined the Committee in 1858, and served on it for nearly 40 years.

Mrs. Barclay, the beloved widow of our dear departed friend, continued to be a succourer of many. She lived mostly at Cromer during her widowhood, and it was a joy and inspiration to me in my work to call and see her, at least once a year, when I visited Cromer on the occasion of the Annual Meeting on behalf of the London City Mission.

MR. JOSEPH HOARE.

Childs Hill House, Hampstead, was the town residence of our beloved Treasurer, Mr. Joseph Hoare, and he often placed it, with its beautiful grounds, at the disposal of the Mission, both for the annual holiday of the missionaries, and also for pleading the cause of the Society. The last occasion was a most memorable one. A large gathering assembled on the lawn to hear some of the most able advocates of the Mission, including the good Lord Shaftesbury. After the company had left I noticed our worthy host chatting cheerfully to Lord Shaftesbury and Mr. J. Fordham as they strolled across the lawn. That was the last time they met on earth, for in the course of a few months all three were called home. Mr. John Fordham went abroad shortly afterwards and died there; Lord Shaftesbury, whose weakness rapidly increased, passed away on the 1st of October, and Mr. Joseph Hoare, who caught a chill at Cromer in the autumn, from which he never recovered, was called home early in January, 1886.

MR. R. C. L. BEVAN.

No place around London was more appreciated by the missionaries and their friends than Trent Park, Barnet, and no heartier welcome did they get from anyone than from its owner, the late Mr. R. C. L. Bevan. I received much help and encouragement from him both as a missionary and also as a District Secretary, and it can truly be said that he loved the Mission, doing all he could to promote its interests. He was the oldest member of its Committee, and one of its most liberal supporters. He joined the Committee in 1841, and for about fifty years took a deep interest in the management of the Society. On seven occasions he received the whole body of missionaries for their annual holiday. For himself, and also for his beloved family, these events were days of joyous service, though fraught with hard toil. By the missionaries he was deservedly loved and honoured, for it was his desire that every missionary should regard him as a personal friend.

It was my happy privilege for several successive years to spend a fortnight in the neighbourhood of Trent Park, and I had some good opportunities of talking to the people around there. After speaking to a man one day about eternal things, while he was at work in his plot—a kind of market garden—I asked him whose land it was on the other side of the hedge.

"Oh," said he, "that belongs to Mr. Bevan, of Trent Park."

"Wouldn't you like a piece out of that to be added to your own; don't you think that he has too much?"

"No," said he, "I don't covet a bit of his land, and I don't think anyone who knows him would do that, nor do I think that anyone around here would hurt a hair of his head, nor let anyone else if they could prevent it. He is a good man and a generous neighbour, and that's saying everything."

MR. R. C. L. BEVAN.

I sometimes took the week evening service at the little Mission Room, and it was customary at the close of the address for one or two of the friends present to offer prayer. One evening, two offered prayer, one a poor old man, dependent on others for his daily bread, and the other was Mr. R. C. L. Bevan. What a sight! Here were a very rich man and a very poor man kneeling at the Throne of Mercy, both confessing their sins before God, both supplicating the mercy of God, both pleading the merit and precious death of Christ for their salvation.

During the latter years of his life Mr. Bevan passed several winters in Cannes, returning in the spring in time for the Society's Annual Meeting in May. He attended the meeting in 1890 for the last time, and was so weak that he had to be almost carried on to the platform, when he received quite an ovation. In the following July, after much patient suffering, he passed peacefully away to his Home above.

MR. AND MRS. F. A. BEVAN.

In the course of time Mr. and Mrs. F. A. Bevan, and family, took up their residence at Trent Park, and continued the traditional hospitality and the philanthropic work of the place. Mr. F. A. Bevan was elected treasurer and chairman of the London City Mission in 1886, after the death of Mr. Joseph Hoare, and it is manifest to all how near the work of the Mission lies to his heart. The whole of the missionaries, as well as the Foreigners' Branch, the Coalies' Branch, and other sections of the Mission, have been entertained most heartily by Mr. and Mrs. F. A. Bevan, at various times, at Trent Park.

MR. THOMAS FOWELL BUXTON.

Mr. Buxton had been connected, more or less, with the London City Mission the whole of his life, for his father, Sir Thomas Fowell Buxton, was the Society's first Treasurer. In fact, many of the various branches of the Buxton family have been good friends and supporters of the Mission, some of them from its commencement.

For many years I had the happy privilege of Christian intercourse with both Mr. and Mrs. Buxton, by letter and personal interviews. As a rule I met them at Cromer in the autumn, and it was encouraging to see the deep interest they took in the work of the Mission. For several years Mr. Buxton had, at different times, represented to me his firm conviction that the Society would accomplish more good if they would employ females as well as males in the work. He asked me to represent his views to the Committee, which I did, when, after consideration, it was felt to be best, at least for the present, to continue to employ only male missionaries.

Mr. Buxton, like many others, had to pass through domestic afflictions and bereavements, and when his beloved wife was called Home in 1905 I ventured to

Photo by]   [J. Russell & Sons.

MR. F. A. BEVAN.

write him a letter of sympathy, and he replied expressing his appreciation of the same, adding, "I am to-day sending the Mission £1,000 'in memory of a beloved wife.'" He only survived Mrs. Buxton three years, as he passed peacefully to his rest on January 27th, 1908—like a ripe sheaf of corn, ready to be garnered—aged 87 years.

I wrote a letter of condolence to the family, and received a very kind reply from his eldest daughter. "The London City Mission," she said, "was as near to his heart as any, and I can remember so well the great interest it always was when the missionaries came to spend their annual day's outing with us as far back as 1856."

Mr. Buxton entertained the Mission on the day of its annual outing on nine different occasions, three at his old residence at Leytonstone, and six at his beautiful place at Easneye, Ware.

A FRIENDSHIP RENEWED.

A very remarkable event took place one day in the East End, which I will notice here.

I heard that Mr. H. Whybrow,* an old friend of mine, had retired from business, and was living at Bow. One morning I was in that neighbourhood and called at his house.

"I had just started to write a letter to you," he said, "about a little money that I should like to give

---

* See page 89.

to your Mission. I have just finished the Mission Hall and residence at Leytonstone, and have put it in Trust for the Society, and I want to know if the Committee will accept a sum of money, upon certain conditions, for the support of a missionary and keeping the place in repair."

In due course all was arranged, and the stock was transferred to the Committee, in the names of the three trustees of the Mission.

He occasionally sent for me to hear about the work of the Mission in which he was intensely interested, particularly the work carried on in the Mission Hall which he had erected and supported.

He once asked me to remain while he made a rough draft of his will. "I will give the Society," he said, "six thousand pounds—subject to a life interest in the same—for I cannot tell you what I owe to the Mission." This and other legacies were drafted, and in due time properly finished. The end came soon after, and the income of the legacy is paid to the young widow during her lifetime. He was a good man and generous to his employees. For over fifty years he was attached to a large Sunday School as teacher and superintendent. He was a diligent student of Holy Scripture, and was ever ready to help the cause of Christ and the poor. He was a most lovable man, and I was drawn to him as a wise counsellor and friend.

MR. T. FOWELL BUXTON.

SIR GEORGE WILLIAMS.

I found a most helpful adviser and friend in that great and good man, Mr., afterwards Sir, George Williams. He was not only a member of the Parent Committee, but also a very helpful member of the North-West London Auxiliary Committee as well as President of several local associations. His house in Russell Square was often placed at the service of the Mission for advocating the claims of the Society, for Committee Meetings, etc., and it would be impossible to tell the blessed results from meetings held in that house.

He was always willing (whenever his many engagements in his busy life permitted him) to preside at meetings in other parts of London, and many valuable supporters in God's work have thereby been enlisted. He was a most warm-hearted and liberal-minded Christian, and I seldom put before him the claims of a needy district, or the sorrows and distress of a deserving family, or individual, without getting help for them. A gentleman, when driving him home after a meeting, said to him, " I wonder that you don't keep a carriage and pair to take you about, Mr. Williams." He replied in his usual smiling way, " Well, you see, I drive a pair of missionaries instead, and it would surprise you to know the amount of joy I get from doing so."

One of the most successful—at least, in its ultimate results—of the meetings held in the house of Sir

George Williams, was that to which Louisa Lady Ashburton was invited. She remained to dinner, and I was invited to stay and tell her more about our work. On leaving she gave me a substantial cheque for the Mission, and desired me to call on her the next day.

LOUISA LADY ASHBURTON.

In response to an invitation, I called upon this lady at Kent House, Knightsbridge, her town house. She asked numerous questions as to the constitution and method of working the Mission, all of which I fully explained. At the close of this interview she kindly promised to support two missionaries, one in the neighbourhood of the church she attended and the other near the docks.

This was the commencement of a friendship which lasted to the end of her life—nearly 20 years. She would often send for me to enquire about the work, and express her desire to do something to help the poor in the great East End to a better life. I suggested various ways in which this could be done. It was finally arranged that I should accompany her to see these neglected parts for herself. She therefore called for me a few days later, at the Mission House, and we drove through the East End, over the Lea River Bridge into Canning Town, and then went about three miles along by the "Victoria and Albert Docks."

She was horrified at the terrible scenes she witnessed in that long main road by the side of the docks. The abject wretchedness and squalor to be seen everywhere, the hundreds and thousands of working men standing about the various entrances to the docks, with the hope of getting a chance day's work, the many well-filled public-houses, the dirty neglected children, with their dissipated looking mothers, made her sad indeed. With tears in her eyes, she exclaimed, "Oh, do help me to do something for these people, will you not, and it will add ten years to my life?" The Committee gave me permission to help her in any way I could.

The next time we went there the horses were put up, and we investigated this same neighbourhood again on foot. No one knew who we were when we entered different shops or public-houses to make certain enquiries.

It was afternoon when we entered the large public-house almost opposite Custom House Station, and it was full of men and women drinking. Her Ladyship crushed in with me, and as she stood among them she seemed quite overcome with grief to see the half-naked shoeless little children among the number. We were shown into a "private parlour," and when the waitress came to know what we required, my friend asked to see the proprietor. After a time he came, and a sharp conversation ensued.

"May I have a little plain talk with you?" her Ladyship asked.

"If you wish, Madam," he replied.

" Were you brought up in this line of business? "

" Oh, no, I was brought up to farming."

" And why did you not keep to that business? "

" Because this pays much better."

" How much do you get a year out of this? "

" Oh, I can't tell you ; do you want to buy it? "

" Well, yes, I might do so ; what do you want for it? "

" Do you mean business, or what is your object in talking to me? "

" I am here for business," she replied.

" If that is so, I should require £20,000 at least for the goodwill of this house, that means, just to walk out and let you take possession as it stands, and a good bargain, too, you would say you had, if you saw my books."

" If I buy it will you give me a promise not to take another public-house, but to go back to farming? "

" No, certainly not.　I should most likely have another house in this neighbourhood."

" Are you happy, and is your conscience easy while witnessing such scenes as I saw in front of your bar to-day? "

" It is not a question of happiness or conscience with me, but of money-making."

She probed him with many more questions which evidently made him feel ill at ease, for he did not like to hear of responsibility, death, and judgment. He asked, would she turn it into some other line of business if she bought it, assuring her it was the very best position in the whole neighbourhood.

As the man seemed intent on striking a bargain, and my friend was evidently leaning that way, I looked at my watch, and starting to my feet said, "We must be going, as we have an engagement now due." I had some little difficulty in getting her out, as I was afraid she would give a cheque as a deposit on the purchase.

As we drove back to town she was full of the idea of purchasing the place, and it was some time before I could dissuade her from it. I assured her we could do much better than paying that large sum for the goodwill of that house. Then she said, "Do the best you can, and as quickly as you can, that these poor men may have a place to go into other than the public-house, but let no one know you are doing it for me."

A START.

I started to work in good earnest and a suitable house was found at the corner of Custom House Terrace. A coal merchant owned it, using the lower part as an office, and after several interviews he agreed to sell it for £700. His wife was most anxious to know to what purpose I was going to put it, and when she heard that it was going to be a centre for Christian effort on behalf of the poor, she said, "You can have it for £600. I will gladly forego £100 to have a Mission Station in this terrible neighbourhood."

The place was converted into a coffee tavern, with

Mission premises upstairs. When all was ready the question arose as to the opening ceremony. My lady friend wished Her Royal Highness, the late Duchess of Teck, to open it, but would it be safe in the midst of such a seething mass of discontents, for there were so many men out of work, among whom were thousands of the so-called dangerous Socialists, who every week paraded the main road to the city boundary in a menacing manner. The question was fully considered, and after consulting with the police authorities it was decided to try it.

ROYALTY AND SOCIALISM.

The true state of affairs was laid before Her Royal Highness, and after much prayer for Divine protection and for a blessing to rest on this effort, she consented to come down and open the premises. We did all we could to ensure a peaceful and happy visit, and the police authorities said they hoped everything would pass off quietly, but they could not be absolutely sure of this. Large placards were displayed in the neighbourhood, and a number of notable persons, friends, and sympathizers were invited. Her Royal Highness, with her charming daughter—the present Princess of Wales—arrived punctually to time, and were received right royally by those assembled in the place, while the teeming mass outside looked sullenly on. After an address to Her Royal Highness was read, the visitors took tea in the coffee room, and amusingly demanded

Photo by]   [Elliott & Fry.

MRS. F. A. BEVAN.

to pay their penny for each cup. It was then declared open to the public.

As Her Royal Highness looked out upon the dense mass of working men in the crowded thoroughfare, she said, '' Who are these crowds of men in the streets? '' I said, '' They are dockers out of work, and are called dangerous Socialists.'' '' Poor men,'' she exclaimed, '' can you arrange for 200 of them to have a good meat tea? If so, I will give it them.''

This being gladly accepted, Lady Ashburton said, '' I will also give the same to 200 men out of work to-morrow night.'' Then Mrs. F. A. Bevan said, '' And I shall be glad to do the same the third night,'' and a local friend said he would do the same on the fourth night. The services of one man was required to accomplish this large order without confusion. By the aid of the police inspector I found him, and after a little talk with him he promised to do all he could to help me, as he knew the men.

And now a remarkable scene followed at which the whole body of police were astounded. After I had announced to the crowd what was going to be done for them, and by whom, on four successive nights, and that their leader—who stood by my side—would see that only those who had no work would get a ticket for the supper, an opening was made for the carriage to take up their Royal Highnesses. As soon as they were seated this most dangerous leader, of a most dangerous class—according to the statement of the police and public—leapt on the wheel of the carriage, and throwing up his cap, called for three cheers for their Royal Highnesses. At this, a shout which startled the whole neighbourhood, went up from a thousand throats, during which the carriage drove off.

Thus began a work for God which grew and developed to marvellous dimensions.

The arrangements for the suppers were carried through most happily, and both the authorities of the law and ladies and gentlemen from the West End said they never saw " dangerous Socialism " get such a blow as it had from this religious and philanthropic effort of her ladyship.

EXPANSION.

It was soon evident that the place was not large enough, either for the accommodation of the men or for the religious work carried on by the City Missionary and other workers. Negotiations were started for the purchase of the three houses adjoining the Mission premises. This was quietly accomplished, the owner not knowing for whom I was buying them. The upper parts were converted into dormitories where men could have a comfortable bed at a reasonable charge. Still further expansion had to be effected, as the evangelistic work was cramped for want of room, so the whole of " Custom House Terrace " was bought, also two houses, one in each side street, behind the Terrace. Three houses in the front were pulled down and a large Mission Hall built, with accommodation for nearly 800 people, with smaller rooms for classes, and quarters for visitors and workers.

I need not speak of the many difficulties which had to be overcome, but they disappeared one after another before believing prayer and persistent effort, and a happy day it was, both to Lady Ashburton and myself, when the Duchess of Teck, who was again accompanied by her daughter, opened the beautiful Hall and other premises, and gave it the name of " The Louisa Ashburton Mission."

A number of wealthy people came from the West End to meet their Royal Highnesses, among them being the Marquis of Northampton and his charming wife, who was the only child of Lady Ashburton.

When the ceremony was over and the company were taking a little refreshment, her Ladyship's daughter, Lady Compton (as she then was), came into a room where I was attending to some duties alone, and said, " Now, Mr. Dunn, will you kindly tell me how this has all been brought about?" I said, " Has your dear mother told you anything about it?" "Oh, yes, she has told me a little, but she says you have had to do it, and you know all." I said, " Yes, I can tell you all about it if you wish. I was pledged to secrecy, but I am free now as regards yourself." I explained all to her; the difficulties, and the encouragements, the apparent failures and the successes, until we had attained that crowning day.

As she stood before me, tall, erect, lovely—for she was a most beautiful woman—listening to all I said, she exclaimed, when I finished, "I cannot tell you how much I rejoice with you, in all I see and hear this day. I do thank God for all He has enabled my dear mother to accomplish here, and I also thank God that you have so well taken care of her and guarded her interests."

Other extensions were made inside the docks for the welfare and comfort of the working men, and the whole of the buildings cost nearly twenty thousand pounds, this amount being defrayed by Lady Ashburton. She greatly rejoiced in the good work that was carried on at this centre of Christian activity, for vast numbers of men in the neighbourhood were won to the Saviour, and they are influencing, not only the mass of ungodly people around, but are witnessing for Christ in ships and ports all over the world.

The place stands out as a great moral and spiritual lighthouse to poor tempest-tossed sin-stricken souls who are found in the docks or ashore. For nearly twenty years her Ladyship was spared to see this good and noble work carried on, and she often said she believed it had added years to her life.

Her ladyship received the Home call in February, 1903, her daughter—Lady Northampton—having pre-deceased her. Changes have taken place which I need not refer to, but the two city missionaries still work in connection with the Hall, and I pray that the work may be perpetuated to future generations, for the glory of God, and as a monument to her memory.

FURTHER CHANGES.

Death has always been the means of bringing about great changes. It was so in what I am about to relate. One of my most esteemed colleagues, Mr. C. M. Sawell, who for many years had been one of the Society's most indefatigable District Secretaries, was called Home, after a short illness. He had been instrumental in raising large sums of money for the work of the Mission, as well as launching forth some new branches of Mission work. Beloved by the whole body of missionaries, who looked upon him as their true friend, he had to lay aside his armour, and the work he had so successfully carried on in the City and Central Auxiliary was given over to me. I had, therefore, to surrender some of the work I had been engaged in. The work of the great "North-West Auxiliary" (with its various "Ladies' Associations" and Committees) was passed over to one of my colleagues. The severance of the tie of such happy Christian fellowship with men and women of God, with whom it had been my privilege to co-operate, was indeed severe.

After the change had been made I received the following resolution from the Committee of the above Auxiliary.

" That the Committee of the N.-W. Auxiliary
" of the London City Mission having learned with

" great regret of the decision of the Parent Society
" to transfer their excellent Secretary, Mr. James
" Dunn, to a larger sphere of usefulness, desire
" to place on record their appreciation of his
" character and work, and of the devotion and
" ability with which he has prosecuted his labours
" during the eleven years he has been associated
" with them.

" While deeply regretting the severance of the
" happy bond, they recognize and acknowledge
" the Divine Hand in the arrangement, and assure
" their friend that they will ever cherish a prayer-
" ful interest in him and his work. They earnest-
" ly trust that God's blessing may abundantly rest
" upon all that he undertakes, and especially in
" connection with the Mission so dear to all our
" hearts, and to which he has so zealously conse-
" crated his life."

Here follows the Signatures of the Committee.

June 16, 1893.

Warren Hall
Chairman

J. K. Singleton

Frederick P. Weaver

George Williams

Chas. T. Bourne

William S. Gard

Ellen J. Brewster

U. A. Tyse

James Arthurton

Expresspekul

William Carter

E. Bird

William Carter

This closed the sixth decade of my life, and while I could not be sufficiently thankful to our gracious God for the blessings and mercies that had followed me all my days, still I began to feel my physical powers for endurance not what they once were. Amid all the changes, sorrows and bereavements through which I have been called to pass, my hope is still in God, and my prayer is :—

" Abide with me : fast falls the eventide ;
   The darkness deepens ; Lord, with me abide :
   When other helpers fail, and comforts flee,
   Help of the helpless, oh, abide with me !

" Swift to its close ebbs out life's little day ;
   Earth's joys grow dim, its glories pass away ;
   Change and decay in all around I see,
   O Thou Who changest not, abide with me !

" I need Thy presence every passing hour ;
   What but Thy grace can foil the tempter's power?
   Who like Thyself my guide and stay can be?
   Through cloud and sunshine, oh, abide with me ! "

SEVENTH DECADE.

In this new department as District Secretary for the City and Central Auxiliary I had to a great extent to adopt new methods in seeking to raise funds. To get the ears of keen rushing business men, such as bankers, merchants, and men in the various large city marts, and others, so as to plead the cause I had at heart, required a deal of caution, and not a little tact and skill. By some I was received courteously, by others I was rebuffed.

Some would say, " Now, Sir, I can only give you two or three minutes, what is it you want? " In such a case I had to compress my request into as few words as possible, and perhaps while I was so doing the gentleman would be called away on some important business question, and I was told I must see him another time.

Gentlemen were sometimes annoyed at my intruding into their presence during business hours, although I found sometimes this was only simulation. Where, however, it appeared real and very determined, an earnest appeal in a Christ-like spirit has sometimes won a person over to our cause.

I was once having a talk with a gentleman who had long been a friend of the Mission, when he said, " I wish I could interest Mr. —— in the work. He is a good sort of man, with plenty of means, and could render you substantial help, and if you call upon him now you will most probably find him in."

Now, I must confess that sometimes when appealing for help I have been politely asked to call on some-one else, merely to get rid of me. One would say, "I fully believe in your work, and only wish I could help you, but you try so-and-so, for he has plenty of money, and no doubt will readily help you." Another would say, "Mr. —— has just made a lot of money, and does not know what to do with it all. I would help you if I was in his position, go and see him, for he *could* help you and would never miss it." Sometimes people to whom I have been thus referred, have said the same things about those who have sent me.

But this does not apply to the following. Entering the outer office of this gentleman, and finding he was within I sent in my card, and after waiting some time he came out and asked my business. I told him that I represented the London City Mission, and said how thankful we should be for any help he could give to enable us to carry on this work of evangelization among the poor of London. In rather severe terms he expressed not only his unwillingness to help, but his inability to do so. He said to me, "How do you know *what* I have to do, and what I am *able* to do? I live a little way out in the country, and I have to do a great deal there, I assure you, in supporting the work of

God, and I can give you nothing for your work in London. I call it an impertinence on your part coming to me in business hours, and I should like to know who told you to call on me."

When he had finished he looked sternly at me, waiting for my reply. I told him I was thankful to hear of the many good works he was engaged in supporting, and should never presume for a moment to say *what* he should do, and, of course, I did not know anything as to his ability; these were questions between himself and God. I suggested that we were both seeking to serve God in our respective spheres, and trusted that we might both receive His approval at last. I apologized for calling during business hours, but I did not know otherwise how I could get to see him. Thanking him for hearing what I had to say, and bidding him good-day, I opened the door to leave, when he called me back and said, "Here, wait a minute." He retired to his room, and in a short time returned with a cheque, saying, "I have much pleasure in giving you this towards your good work, and, after all, I am glad you called."

APPEARANCES.

I found that my appearance in dress affected people upon whom I called in different ways. Perhaps wearing a round jacket and soft felt hat I would call upon a city gentleman, and he would give me gentle hints that my attire was scarcely suitable, or might more plainly say that I ought to come in a frock coat and silk hat. When, however, I called upon another gentleman in the frock coat and silk hat he said, "Why, Mr. D——, you look by your appearance as though you had a very lucrative position, you dress better than I do." I answered I should be most happy to appear before him in whatever attire he preferred, if only I could meet his wishes. After enquiring about our work and its needs he was quite confident that it was the very thing that was wanted to supplement the efforts of the churches. He gave me a guarantee towards the support of two districts, and was deeply grieved when through some sad reverses he could no longer continue to do so.

I met a number of Christian men in the different metropolitan markets who were much interested in our work, and they not only helped it themselves, but sought to enlist the sympathies of others. Mark Lane had a "prayer union," and I sometimes attended to give an address on our work amongst the poor, which resulted in funds being raised for the support of the work, and several gentlemen became local superintendents. Not only in Mark Lane Market, but also in Billingsgate, Leadenhall, and Smithfield Markets were the sympathy and support of Christian friends secured. The Society had also some valuable friends on the Stock Exchange, the Coal Exchange, the large Banking Houses, etc., and I will now give a short account of the connection with the Mission of two sincere friends.

MR. B. M. TITE.

It is many years ago since I first met Mr. B. M. Tite, who was a member of the Coal Exchange and also on the Committee of the Hackney and Clapton Association when I was appointed District Secretary to that part of London. After a drawing-room meeting in that district had been held, at which he was present, he asked me to call and see him at his home in Clapton, when he told me how his soul was troubled about the spiritual condition of the men engaged in the coal trade of London.

"It is something terrible to contemplate," he said, "the awful condition of the working men who are engaged in our trade, when we send out the vans of coal we can never be sure when the men will return. Now, several of us (merchants) are seriously concerned about this state of things, as it certainly seems to be getting worse, so I suggested that if we could get a suitable City Missionary, one who would understand these rough men, and could bring the Gospel to bear on their hearts and consciences, it would, doubtless, improve these things. Can you appoint a man to this work if I give you a guarantee towards his support?"

It was this interview which led to the formation of the "Mission to Coalies and Carmen, in connection with the London City Mission," which has been so richly owned and blessed of God, that at the present time there are six missionaries at work among the coalies.

MR. JOHN MARNHAM.

I had known Mr. Marnham for many years, but I became more intimately acquainted with him on taking over the City Auxiliary. For many years he was a member of the Stock Exchange, and had been elected Chairman of the same. He used to tell me of the goodness of God and of His providential dealings with him, ever since, as a poor youth, he came to London to find his way in the world. He was a subscriber to our Mission for nearly fifty years. In 1880 he gave the full support for one missionary in our Mission, and at that time he was elected a member of the Parent Committee. In a few years' time he undertook the support of a second missionary, and being their local superintendent he had weekly interviews with them, from which, he said, he derived much joy and strength from united fellowship and prayer. In 1895, support having failed for a district, he again came forward and undertook to support a third missionary, which he continued till his death, which took place in 1903, and bequeathed a sum sufficient to continue the work for some years to come.

In seeking to obtain financial help from the City Corporation and Livery Companies they could only be reached by "Petition," when they would sometimes vote grants of money of various amounts. For some years past the Lord Mayor—for the time being—has kindly convened a meeting at the Mansion House, where the work of the Mission has been made known and new friends and support obtained.

THE FOREIGNERS' BRANCH.

It was during this period that I was appointed the Secretary of this Branch. It had its own Committee and constitution, but was subject to the Parent Society. Its object was to evangelize the various nationalities in London, or those who came to her port as sailors, etc. It employed about twenty agents, to Jews, Germans, French, Italians, Scandinavians, Asiatics, Africans, etc., and they could proclaim the Gospel in about twenty languages. It would be impossible to tell the far-reaching blessings that have attended these efforts. Men have been converted here who have been bearers of the glad message to the ends of the earth. I have had the privilege of visiting several places in Europe, and have there met persons who were witnessing for Christ, having been brought to know the Truth in London by the efforts of our missionaries. In several towns in France and Italy, where I spent a holiday in company with the missionary to Italians in London, I was delighted to find so many people who recognized him as being their friend and spiritual instructor when they were in London.

Some, who were almost destitute when the missionary first met them, are now in good positions, and still they look upon the missionary as their friend.

Many years ago an Italian youth found himself—

like many another youth—stranded in London without money or friends. Hungry and ill-clad he found out the missionary, who, after a long talk with him in the Mission Room, gave him food and lodging for the night. The missionary then called on a lady friend who was always willing to help distressed cases as far as possible, and related his sad story. She listened and then asked what his occupation was. The missionary replied, "He is a modeller." A sister of the lady being present, said, "Let him come and take a model of my foot, and if it is any good I will pay him something."

The missionary hurried back bearing the good news, and rigged him out in decent clothes suitable to appear before the ladies the next morning. The youth, having procured the necessary materials, found his way to the lady's house, with a glad heart, and moulded the young lady's foot. When he had finished the model it was found to be so perfect that it was the means of procuring him plenty of work. When the "Pear's Soap" firm offered a large sum for the best design for advertising their soap, he modelled the well known "You dirty boy," and received the first place. After this his fame rose rapidly, and in the course of time he made his fortune and retired from business to live in his native country (Italy). He remembers the missionary who helped him in London, and is always glad to see or hear from him.

The missionaries to foreigners in London have, for

some years now, been invited to spend a day in the country, with a contingent of their respective nationalities. For several years past this honour has been shared between Mr. and Mrs. Robert Barclay and Mr. and Mrs. F. A. Bevan.

THE AYAHS' HOME.

For many years there had been a home for these sailor nurses in London, kept by a man and his wife, but as they could not make it pay they were about to give it up. The matron saw me to ascertain if the London City Mission would take the place over. I submitted the proposal to the Committee, and the Home was ultimately acquired. The premises, which were located in a most wretched neighbourhood, were so entirely unsuitable to the requirements of a Home for Indian women, that a far better place was found in King Edward Road, Hackney, where the work is still carried on.

OLD COLLEAGUES PASSING.

I always feel something of loneliness when old comrades, with whom I have worked harmoniously for nearly forty years, are called away. During this period of my life several were called Home.

Mr. John Matthias Weylland had been connected with the London City Mission for nearly fifty years, and was most successful both as a missionary and also for about twenty-five years of that time as a District

Secretary. His health had been failing for some time, and on the 4th October, 1897, he received his Home call.

I visited him for the last time on a Sunday afternoon, a few hours before he yielded up his spirit into the hands of his Saviour. The family, gathered to watch their loved one depart, said, " He is unconscious now, he has not recognized any of us for some time, but we should like you to speak to him." I did so, and he responded, " My—friend. I'm—nearly—home." Looking upwards and raising his hands, he said, " Come—Lord—Jesus—take—me—home." By the radiant glow on his features it was evident that he saw visions which were withheld from us. He again opened his eyes, and held out his hand, which I took in mine. I softly said, " This is the Sabbath evening, and I am going to try and preach to some five hundred people, have you a message for me to take to them?" He said at intervals, " The—spirit—and the—bride—say —come." " Tell it—out—spread—it—abroad." After a pause, his hand still in mine, with a dying grip he said, " Good—night—farewell." I replied, " We'll meet in the morning." " Yes—in—the—morning," he said, feebly, as I laid his hand down. This was his last adieu.

Mr. Hugh Pearson had served the Mission for fifty years, half that time as a missionary, and the latter part as a District Secretary. In 1893 his powers began to-fail, and he felt that the time had come when he should retire. He lived for two years after giving up his work, and passed away in July, 1895, after a few days' illness. I had known him intimately ever since I joined the Mission, and was closely in touch with him since being appointed a District Secretary, and we were near neighbours in our residences.

For forty-five years he usually conducted two services weekly at the "Elizabeth Fry Refuge," and when he passed away the Committee of that Institution asked me to take up the duties, which I have had much pleasure in continuing up to the present time.

Mr. James Rennie joined the Mission as one of the General Superintendents a little while before I became a missionary, and we worked together for thirty years. He had remarkably good health, but thirty years' labour among the courts and alleys of East London told on his strong constitution, and in June, 1895, he resigned. Mr. Rennie lived eight years after his retirement, and passed away in August, 1903, at the advanced age of eighty-three. As he resided near my home I frequently called upon him, and his enquiries about the work of the Mission showed how near it lay to his heart. Some time before his death his powers gradually failed, and he requested me to read and pray with him, as often as I could, which gave me much joy. He retained consciousness to the last, and his end was most peaceful.

SIR GEO. WILLIAMS, KT.

DEATH OF SIR GEORGE WILLIAMS.

I have noticed in an earlier part of the book what a warm friend we had in this great worker for God, and it only remains now for me to notice his strong attachment to the work of the London City Mission, and his peaceful end and burial.

In 1894, the Jubilee year of the Y.M.C.A., the Queen offered to Mr. George Williams—shortly before the date fixed for the Jubilee—the honour of knighthood in acknowledgment of his " distinguished service to the cause of humanity." This honour was one of the most popular tributes of modern times, for the news was received with acclamation, not only in England, but in every nation in Europe.

As Sir George Williams attained the age of four score years his powers appeared to be gradually giving way. For several years he spent the winter in the Riviera, but in his eighty-fourth year he was persuaded by his doctors to abandon his usual winter trip, and he went to Torquay instead.

In November, 1905, his family were summoned, and in the evening of the day he slept to wake no more in this world. His remains were laid to rest in St. Paul's Cathedral on the 14th of November, beloved and mourned by vast multitudes. Deputations from about one hundred different societies with which our late friend had been connected, filled the vast Temple, including the officers and one hundred missionaries from the London City Mission.

For myself, I can only add that by the death of Sir George Williams I lost a warm-hearted helper and counsellor in my work.

DEATH OF REV. ROBERT DAWSON, B.A.

For twenty-five years Mr. Dawson had filled the post of Secretary—conjointly with the Rev. T. S. Hutchinson, M.A.—but for some time before the end came his health had been failing, still he clung to his much loved work, until he was compelled to relinquish it and enter a nursing home. He gradually sank from weakness of the heart, and peacefully passed away to be with Christ, on March 20th, 1906. He had attended the funeral of Sir George Williams, with us, but his extreme weakness was manifest then, and in about four months after that event he was called to higher service.

I could say a great deal of our dear friend's devotion of heart and service of life, but that has already been done in the Society's Magazine, after his decease, and I also referred to it in my former little book, " Modern London."

CONCLUSION.

The seventh decade of my life is closing, and as I take a final review I must exclaim, " Surely goodness and mercy have followed me all the days of my life." What experiences I have passed through, and what changes have I seen during the fifty years that I have known London. Its population has increased about six-fold, its extent has grown tremendously, its means of transit from point to point, compared with the old methods of travelling, are most marvellous. The social and spiritual condition of the people is also far different from what it was half a century ago; for while there is still much to cause the true follower of Christ sadness and sorrow of heart as he beholds the poverty and sin of such vast numbers of its teeming population, much of the crass ignorance, and rough brutal conduct of those early days has gone, we hope, never to return.

I am no longer young. I have passed the meridian of life, and have reached the "allotted span," and I desire, with all sincerity of heart, to bear my humble testimony to the faithfulness of God, and the all-sufficient, sustaining power and Divine consolation of His Holy Word. It is nearly fifty years since, convinced that I was a hell-deserving sinner, I took my Bible and sought salvation therein. It led me to Christ as the One and only appointed Saviour.

I have told in these pages of some of the many spiritual contests in which I have engaged, with no other weapon but the Sword of the Spirit; I have told of some of the glorious victories it has won, and now that my sun is hastening to the western sky, I want, from the depths of my being, to commend it to all. It is a source of strength that knows no weakness, a light that never grows dim, a star that never wanes, a sun that never sets; it directs to the fountain of Life, which defies death. I loved to peruse its sacred pages when I was young, and now I am old and grey, it is my staff and stay; I will still trust and not be afraid. " Yea, though I walk through the valley of the shadow of death, I will fear no evil; for Thou art with me; Thy rod and Thy staff, they comfort me." The children's hymn on the Bible is suitable to old age, and so I will say and sing :—

" Holy Bible, Book Divine,
　　Precious treasure, thou art mine."

What shall I say of Him Who is the " Alpha and Omega " of the Book—the Lord Jesus Christ? As

He was when I first saw Him as my dying Saviour and Lord, "the chiefest among ten thousand, the altogether lovely," "the faithful and true witness"; so He has been to me all along the journey, and as that journey is nearing its end, He is more precious to me than ever.

To trust Jesus Christ as a personal, almighty ,and ever-living Saviour, most assuredly brings peace, comfort and joy. The great loving heart of Jesus is what every sin-stricken and sorrowing penitent sinner needs, and when he responds to His loving invitation, " Come unto Me, all ye that labour and are heavy laden, and I will give you rest," he finds a Heart that beats in sympathy with his own.

Around the Person of Jesus Christ gather the doctrines of our holy religion, which I firmly hold and never cease to teach. They are set forth in the " constitution " of the London City Mission, and are given " not in the words which man's wisdom teacheth, but which the Holy Ghost teacheth." " All have sinned and come short of the glory of God." " In the beginning was the Word, and the Word was with God, and the Word was God, and the Word was made flesh, and dwelt among us." " Except a man be born again, he cannot see the Kingdom of God." " The Blood of Jesus Christ, God's Son, cleanseth us from all sin." " Being justified by faith, we have peace with God through our Lord Jesus Christ." " Neither is there

Q

salvation in any other; for there is none other name under heaven given among men, whereby we must be saved." " Without holiness no man shall see the Lord." " Ye are sanctified . . . . by the Spirit of our God."

With my whole heart I subscribe to these Divine truths, for the Lord Himself taught them all, and I would beseech any wavering souls who may read these lines—as though it were my dying testimony for Christ and Truth—to turn their eyes to the crucified One, to accept the declaration concerning Him, for He is the " Teacher sent from God."

I am thankful to be permitted to continue still in the service of our Lord. It has been a most happy, delightful, joyous service to me. In looking back over the years, since I was first called to the work, I can truly see very much done that should not have been done, and very much more left undone that should have been done; and my very best needs cleansing in the Atoning Blood. I lay myself and my unworthy service at the feet of our Divine Lord, and plead His merits as the only ground of my hope and acceptance.

Now, to God the Father, Who hath led me all my days, to God the Son, my Redeemer and Advocate, and to God the Holy Ghost, Who hath sustained and comforted me in all my conflicts and sorrows—to the Triune God—I ascribe all praise, honour, and glory. " I shall be satisfied, when I awake, with Thy likeness."

"O sweet abode of peace and love,
  Where pilgrims freed from toil are blessed,
Had I the pinions of a dove,
  I'd fly to thee and be at rest.
But, hush, my soul, nor dare repine;
  The time my God appoints is best;
While here, to do His will be mine;
  And His, to fix my time to rest."

Suckling & Co., Printers, 88, Fleet Street, London, E.C.

THE
LONDON CITY MISSION:
Instituted 1835.
ITS RISE AND WORK.
By the late I. M. WEYLLAND.

UPON a visit to Dublin I was requested to address a meeting about the work of the London City Mission. At the close, an aged man, leaning upon an oaken stick, came up to me and said, "Let me shake hands with you, as my heart is full of gratitude to Almighty God, for He did it in answer to prayer. I will tell you all about it. Well, I was a young fellow then, and went with my parents to the prayer-meeting. We had all been reading about London going to the bad—a third of its people living heathen lives, with rookeries crowded with violent and criminal men and women. The new police were invented, but they could only go in groups into these places, and no good came of it, as the people were like savages, being ignorant, drunken, and desperate. The minister talked about it, and told us to pray that the Christians of London might be brought to unite in taking the Gospel to the people as the only remedy; and we did pray hard, I can tell you, Mr. Parnell—afterwards Lord Congleton—leading us. Now, we had a young man named David Nasmith, who came from Glasgow, to help our minister. After the closing hymn, several ladies went up to him, and said, 'You must go to London, David, and bring the Christians, who are quarrelling over their Reform Bill, together, and set them to work in effort to save the people.' 'I would like to go,' he said, ' but expenses—only the necessary ones—will be great, and I have no money.' Then the few who remained talked the matter over, and before lights were put out, the ladies (and mother was one of them) had promised to raise £100 a year for the purpose, and David had promised to go. Praise the Lord!" exclaimed the old man. "All the good done, and 500* men at work—God be praised."

We will continue the narrative, and describe the commencement of the London City Mission :—

Upon his arrival in London, Nasmith engaged a cottage of four rooms, and of low rent, beside the canal in Hoxton. For three weeks he visited poor neighbourhoods in various parts of the City, and even, like Nehemiah of old (*Neh.* ii. 12), contemplated by night the sad ruin of poor humanity in this our Jerusalem. He then went to its chief pastor—the Bishop of London—informed him about the object of his visit to his diocese, and submitted for his approval a constitution for the proposed Mission. His lordship listened to him kindly, and said in reply, "The object is good, but a scheme uniting Nonconformists and Churchmen cannot succeed, and I must withhold my sanction."†

Nothing daunted by this difficulty, he then went to Dr. Campbell, the leading Nonconformist, presented his papers, and explained the details. The doctor promised to consider the matter, and on the next Sunday referred to it in his sermon. He said, "In the present state of feeling between Churchmen and Dissenters, it is impossible to unite them in one Society, however needful and desirable. It is obvious to all who know anything of the working of human

---

* This was the number at the time these words were spoken, but owing to financial necessities, the staff has since been reduced.

† It is gratifying to be able to record that after the lapse of some years, his Lordship gave proof of his appreciation of the Mission, and that for many years one of the Secretaries has been licensed by the Bishop of London to plead the cause of the Society in any Church in his Diocese.

nature in organized societies that an institution so formed cannot become stable and effective." Our visitor then spent several weeks in calling upon leading clergymen, ministers, and laymen; but, while wishing him well, not one of them would join in the movement. "They all with one consent began to make excuse."

The arm of flesh had failed, but David wrote to a friend, "I am not cast down, as I carry with me the Divine warrant and command; and, leaning on His help, I am going forward."

Now it so happened that he met with two men, as poor as himself, who entered with zeal into his plan; and as they could not be absent from their callings by day, they arranged to meet in his little parlour at six o'clock in the morning, on the 16th of May, 1835, for prayer and conference. The power of the Lord was upon them, as they felt constrained to act then and there. So, rising from their knees, David Nasmith proposed, "That we who are now present form ourselves into a Society, to be called the London City Mission." This was seconded by Mr. R. E. Dear, and supported by Mr. W. Bullock. A constitution was then read, and agreed to; a few small coins were placed upon the table, that its treasury might be opened; and then, in solemn prayer, they committed the infant Society to the special blessing and care of Almighty God.

A great event had occurred in the silence and calm of that early morning. The principle of Christian unity had been asserted, and in a marvellous way was to prove its power—even its Divine energy. Many Christians of the City, while holding Christ the Head, and His pure Gospel, had grown cold and distant to each other, and needed to be drawn together and reminded of the departing Saviour's prayer—"that they all may be one; as Thou, Father, art in Me, and I in Thee, that they also may be one in Us: that the world may believe that Thou hast sent Me."

The Committee faced the difficulties before them with

holy determination, meeting several times weekly, at six o'clock in the morning, adding with care to their number. Nasmith devoted his time to writing and circulating information, and in effort to gain helpful friends. Proofs of the Divine favour were given, as Vice-Admiral Vernon Harcourt, son of the Archbishop of York, became an active member of Committee, and Sir Thomas Fowell Buxton, who was then pleading the cause of the slave in the senate of England, became Treasurer. At once the Society leaped into public favour. Men of the right stamp, with burning zeal and knowledge of the people, offered themselves for the service, while money flowed into its treasury. Districts were surveyed, and appointments rapidly made, and it was then decided to call an inaugural meeting. This was held on the 17th of December, 1835, in the Music Hall, Store Street.

Though as early as eleven o'clock in the morning, a dense crowd thronged the hall, and a holy enthusiasm pervaded the assembly, the meeting lasting five hours. At that gathering of Christians it may be said that "the rose, the shamrock, and the thistle were bound together by the cords of love in the Spirit." The Rev. the Hon. Baptist Noel, who was in the chair, as an Englishman for England, thanked the Christians of Ireland for sending the Scotsman at his side as their ambassador, and expressed his belief that "the new mission would become a power by which the United Kingdoms, with united believers of every name, would work together for the recovery of the ignorant and debased masses of their common capital." "Domestic chaplains for the people," exclaimed Dr. Leifchild, "that is our meaning, passing from room to room until every individual in the crowded slums has heard the message." "It is related in ancient story," said Dr. Cumming, "that as soon as the rays of the morning sun struck on the brow of the statue of Memnon, the image emitted the most delightful sounds; but in a true and exalted sense, when the rays of the Sun of Righteousness fall on the inhabitants of the heathen districts of the Metropolis, there will arise, not worldly minstrelsy or heathen song, but the voice of joy and the sound of thanksgiving and praise."

After this inaugural gathering such rapid progress was made that on its first anniversary, a year from the early morning when the three feeble disciples met for prayer, *forty-one* Missionaries were penetrating the lowest parts of the vast city, publishing with devotion and zeal the message of redeeming mercy. The Lord had wrought wonderfully by His servants, with indications of yet greater blessings.

The way being thus prepared, the Missionaries pressed forward in their work with quiet energy, avoiding all matters contentious and political. Their instructions were, "Go to the district assigned you, make the acquaintance of every man, woman, and child with the one object of bringing them to a knowledge of salvation by our Lord Jesus Christ, doing them good by every means in your power." As these districts were small, containing about 500 families each, there was no waste of time, and every individual was soon known, the sick frequently visited, and the children gathered into ragged and Sunday schools. Then a room was engaged, and frequent meetings held for reading the Scriptures and prayer that the rightly impressed might be prepared to attend the house of the Lord. One incident will illustrate the working of this system.

A strong young man from a Kentish village was appointed to Angel Gardens—a maze of courts and alleys with high tumble-down houses. After a few hours' visiting, he was hounded out by a furious mob, as he was suspected of being a detective. Next day, he returned to the charge, explained his office, and gained access to some people who were ill. As all the inhabitants were criminal and depraved, his life at times was in danger. One woman kicked at his face from a landing, and he was struck at by several men. Opposition was bravely encountered, until two young men thieves were led to leave the den in which they lived, and obtained work, and a girl who had been decoyed into the "Gardens" was placed in a home.

Next day, he was surrounded by a hostile mob, and several foreign sailors brandished their knives. A stout, middle-aged Irishwoman rushed forward with clenched fists, and from the side of the Missionary threatened vengeance to anyone who dared to strike him, as she exclaimed, "And sure he could do good to the likes of us." Giving them time to cool down, the unwelcome visitor returned a few days after, and found that his Irish defender had that same night been taken in charge for having stolen jewellery in her possession. She was transported for five years. Upon her discharge, the Missionary was in the Gardens to receive her, and thank her for defending him in the time of peril. During her absence, a wonderful change had passed over the people. Though many were still desperately wicked, all received the Missionary as a friend, a few of their number being Christianized. Two large rooms had been thrown into one as a hall for Scripture reading and prayer, and this was usually crowded, a ragged school for children being also held in it. As years passed on, the neighbourhood became changed, many souls being gathered into the church of the redeemed.

About 300 Missionaries are thus engaged upon districts, evangelizing among all classes of the poor with wonderful proofs of blessing.

As the Mission gained power, need was found for special effort among various classes of the people, as for instance, the foreigners resident in East London, or connected with its port. The docks were crowded with ships under various flags, and thousands of men from every nation and tongue trod our English shore, and lived for months under the shadow of our churches, returning to their own dark lands without a knowledge of the only true God and Jesus Christ whom He has sent.

One winter morning, a young Missionary saw a group of people round the body of a lascar, who had been frozen to death. "Died here without the knowledge of Christ," he thought, and from that time an effort was made to teach the foreigners who crowded his district. Out of compassion for Asiatics whom he found destitute, he acquired a knowledge of Hindustani, and, in time, of other Eastern tongues, and was appointed Missionary to Orientals. Other appointments were made to people of various nationalities, including French, Germans, and Italians. This Mission has indeed developed into an important *Foreign Missionary Society*, as the Bible is read, and the Gospel message made known by a staff of well-qualified men who teach in the leading languages of the earth. Now visitors from Eastern lands hear in their own tongue the saving fame of Him whose day-star and whose glory rose in the East; and the knowledge of the great salvation is made to spread from our island to the ends of the earth.

The early Missionaries soon found that public-houses, thickly placed in every neighbourhood, and open day and night, were the chief hindrances to the upraising of the people. Encouraged by the Vicar, a Missionary boldly entered all the public-houses in his parish, with such good results that he was appointed to the whole of the 400 public-houses in the parish of Marylebone, with the night dens. This work extended from parish to parish, so that at the present time about eight thousand of the public-houses of London are entered by a staff of skilled Missionaries. These become the friends of the landlords, and while in their bars and tap-rooms they reason with crowds of men and women about righteousness, temperance, and judgment. The drunken and depraved are met on their own ground and helped to a better life, while all sorts and conditions of men listen to truths which concern their salvation. The work is rich in narratives of grace, for which we give thanks continually.

Appointments to special classes gradually became an effective, and increasing part of the Society's labours. The depraved people, such as thieves and outcasts, have always been grappled with, but the respectable working classes, among whom is much ignorance and infidelity, now receive spiritual care. Workshops, factories, and gasworks are visited. Sons of consolation devote their lives to the suffering in the great hospitals, under the directions of the chaplains; while men in the full activities of life are influenced to godliness and virtue. Omnibus and tramcar men have special care, while soldiers, sailors, postmen and sorters, have their own Missionaries, who understand their trials and habits of life. The police, for instance, and our Missionaries have ever been fast friends. That fine body of City police has its own Missionary, who makes acquaintance with the young constables, holds meetings for Scripture reading and prayer in the stations before they go out on duty, and visits the sick at their homes. All the divisions of the force through the vast capital are grateful, and often give proof of their regard. The constables of Bethnal Green, for instance, gave a writing desk, and a testimonial in the form of an illuminated address, to their Missionary upon his retirement. This latter was composed, written, and emblazoned by members of the force.*

Marvellous is the result of that Dublin prayer meeting, and the one in the early morning in the cottage by the canal. It is one of the thousand historic proofs that prayer has power with the Almighty Jehovah.

---

* The Mission has now only one Special Missionary to the Police, who visits those in the City, but the Metropolitan Police are visited by the Missionaries in whose districts the stations are situated.

"Valiant for the Truth."

(A deeply interesting Narrative.)

The Autobiography of the late

J. M. WEYLLAND

(Author of "The Man with the Book," &c.)

Edited by G. HOLDEN PIKE.

With an introduction by the Rev. P. B. POWER, M.A.

PRICE 2/6 POST PAID.

Pioneer Work in the Great City:

The Autobiography of a London City Missionary.

By JOHN HUNT.

With an Introduction by the ARCHDEACON OF LONDON.

CLOTH GILT. ILLUSTRATED. 281 PAGES.
PRICE 1s. 6d. POST PAID.

"It is the very romance of Home Missions."—*Christian.*
"Interesting and instructive."—*Family Churchman.*
"Full of interest from beginning to end."—*Freeman.*
"A record of a remarkable life."—*English Churchman.*

OF ALL BOOKSELLERS.

Wm. GREEN, 3, Bridewell Place, E.C.

TRUFFLE and NEPHEWS.

By the late
Rev. P. B. POWER, M.A.

Forty-One Pages.   Eighteen Illustrations by FRANK BARNARD.

White Leatherette Cover, price **6d.** post paid.

"It is not a new book, but it deserves to be regarded as *ever new*; both for its own worth and for the noble philanthropic purpose with which it was written."—*The News, August 19th, 1904.*

WM. GREEN, 3, Bridewell Place, E.C.

www.ingramcontent.com/pod-product-compliance
Lightning Source LLC
Chambersburg PA
CBHW080550090426
42735CB00016B/3201